SHIPWRECKS
OF THE
CALIFORNIA
COAST

SHIPWRECKS
OF THE
CALIFORNIA
COAST

WOOD TO IRON, SAIL TO STEAM

MICHAEL D. WHITE

Charleston   London

THE
History
PRESS

Published by The History Press
Charleston, SC 29403
www.historypress.net

Front cover: The rusting remains of the Waterman Steamship freighter *Chickasaw*, lost on Santa Rosa Island in 1962. *Courtesy of Robert Schwemmer.*

Back cover: The *Frank Jones* on the rocks near Fort Point, March 30, 1877. *Courtesy of the San Francisco Maritime NHP.*

Back cover, inset: Ashore near Santa Cruz Light, the steam schooner *La Feliz*, ashore and wrecked, October 1, 1924. *Courtesy of the Pacific Grove Museum of Natural History.*

First published 2014

Manufactured in the United States

ISBN 978.1.60949.924.2

Library of Congress CIP data applied for.

CONTENTS

ACKNOWLEDGEMENTS

Anything new is built on a foundation of what has gone before. This book is no different, and it could not have become a reality without a heavy reliance on the works published over the years by others so committed to preserving California's maritime history.

I speak particularly of James Gibbs, Jerry MacMullen, Joe Williamson, James Delgado, Robert Schwemmer, Stephen Haller, James Shaw, William Worden, Charles Regal, Elmar Baxter, John Haskell Kemble, Gordon Newell, John Niven, Steve Potash, Ernest Marquez, Walter Jackson, Fred Stindt, Richard Benson, James Hitchman, JoAnn Semones, Thomas Layton, Harry Kirwin and Don B. Marshall.

I thank them for their work, and my sincere gratitude also goes out to the following for their encouragement and invaluable assistance in compiling the information and images for this book: Gina Bardi, reference librarian, and Ted Miles, assistant reference librarian, at the San Francisco Maritime National Historical Park; Joan Berman, special collections librarian, Humboldt State University Library, Arcata, California; Carolyn Zeitler, archivist at the Kelley House Museum, Mendocino, California; marine archaeologist and historian Robert Schwemmer; Paul Vandecarr, collections curator at the Pacific Grove Museum, Pacific Grove, California; Amanda Williford, curator and reference archivist at the Golden Gate NRA Park Archives & Records Center, San Francisco, California; and Robert W. Graham, archivist of the Historical Collections of the Great Lakes at Bowling Green State University, Bowling Green, Ohio.

I would also like to thank the reference library staffs of the Pasadena Public Library, the Long Beach Public Library, the Burbank Public Library and the Los Angeles Central Library, as well as Courtney A. White, Bruce Roberts and John Penn for their generous assistance in gathering material for this book.

Also due for more than a fair share of praise is the tireless staff responsible for compiling the priceless California Digital Newspaper Collection at the University of California, Riverside's Center for Bibliographical Studies and Research. Their dedicated work in archiving decades of heretofore almost inaccessible California newspapers greatly eased the research that went into this book.

My sincere gratitude also goes out to Jerry Roberts and Will Collicott of The History Press for their encouragement and guidance during the process of piecing this book together.

Lastly, I want to thank my wife, Pamalee, for her support during the yearlong challenge of researching and writing this book. It would not have become a reality without her patience, forbearance and generous spirit, and it is to her that I dedicate this work.

INTRODUCTION

Over the past four centuries, as California morphed from a remote colonial backwater into an almost irresistible magnet for both people and commerce from all over the world, the number of ships sailing its waters grew, as did the number of ships in distress, evidenced by disaster after disaster that claimed thousands of lives and millions of dollars in treasure and cargo.

Exactly how many vessels have been wrecked on that particularly perilous shore over the past four centuries, no one will ever know. Some were famous for their elegant accommodations or admired for their speed, while the majority of others labored as virtually anonymous, unheralded workhorses whose doom on some bleak, rocky point garnered only a fleeting mention on the shipping page of a newspaper. One of the former was the side-wheeler *Tennessee*, inbound for San Francisco from Panama, when she went aground and was wrecked in a dense fog at Indian Cove (later named Tennessee Cove) just four miles from the Golden Gate. The story of the wreck filled hundreds of column inches in newspapers across the country for weeks after the ship went ashore and was wrecked on March 6, 1853.

According to the contemporary history *The Annals of San Francisco*, the graceful *Tennessee* "went upon a small sandy beach, on both sides of which at a short distance, were enormous cliffs, on which, if the vessel struck, she would have gone immediately to pieces, and probably most of those on board would have perished."

Her passengers safely ashore, the ship's crew joined salvors to discharge what part of the cargo and sacks of mail could be saved. It was work, wrote the *Daily Alta California*, that made "her officers and crew feel as if they were attending the funeral obsequies of a dear and valued friend. She was a favorite craft and one of the best sea boats that plowed the Pacific Ocean." The *Tennessee*, the article continued, "was the home, the pride, the refuge of her officers and crew, and many a tear as salt as the brine that surrounds her shattered hull has coursed unhidden from manly eyes and sprung up involuntarily from the bold and courageous hearts of those whose pride and delight she was, as they have gazed upon the last resting place of the gallant *Tennessee*."

A few days later, the *Sacramento Daily Union* reported, "A voluntary meeting of the passengers of the steamship *Tennessee* passed resolutions acquitting Captain Edward Mellus of all blame connected with her loss. They also pay him a high compliment for his zeal, strict attention and noble and gentlemanly conduct on the occasion."

In November 1885, the *Daily Alta California* reported, "It has been a month of hurricanes and heavy seas and some of the staunchest vessels have succumbed to the fierce battle of the elements." The newspaper, the most widely circulated in the state, catalogued the month's losses: the schooner *Hannah Madison*, wrecked at Navarro; the schooners *Mendocino* and *Fairy Queen*, wrecked on the rocks at Whitesboro; and the *Annie Gee*, lost at the mouth of the Elk River.

Ships severely damaged that month alone along the northern coast included the schooners *Lottie Carson*, *Fannie Dutard*, *Maxim* and *Lizzie Madison*; the steamer *Oregon*; and the schooner *Fidelity*, whose master later said the gale in November 1885 "was the worst and heaviest blow he'd ever experienced on this coast."

Hardly in the *Tennessee*'s league, the schooner *J.H. Congdon* was a "butter boat"—an unheralded, two-masted workhorse owned by a cooperative of dairy farmers to haul their products from the tiny coastal town of Bodega south to San Francisco. She was lost, along with all of her crew, on March 31, 1886.

Two days later, a matter-of-fact, single-sentence article appeared in the *Daily Alta California*: "A dispatch was received on Wednesday last at the Merchant's Exchange to the effect that the schooner *J.H. Congdon*, commanded by Capt. Alexander Nelson, bound for San Francisco from Bodega, had capsized off Point Reyes and that no signs had been discovered of her crew."

From 1887 to 1897, an average of one vessel was lost every 2 miles along the 195-mile strip of shoreline between the U.S. Life-Saving Stations at Point Arena and Humboldt Bay. That averages out to almost ten ships lost on that stretch of coast every year of that decade.

Since official record keeping began in the mid-nineteenth century, the fog-shrouded granite rocks of Point Reyes have claimed more than fifty ships, while almost three dozen sailing schooners, brigs, barks, clippers, steamers, tankers, freighters and steam schooners have met their fate on the Seal Rocks below the Cliff House, near the mouth of San Francisco Bay.

In 1894 alone, a full dozen ships were wrecked on Point Bonita near the mouth of the Golden Gate. And the U.S. Department of Commerce calculated that from 1900 to 1917, sixty-two ships were stranded or wrecked on the California coastline. Four of them were lost within thirty-six hours (September 4–5, 1904) when they went ashore in a dense fog "that fell like a pall" at the entrance to San Francisco Bay: the three-masted schooner *James A. Garfield*, the British-flag iron ship *Drumburton*, the steamer *Newberg* and the steam schooner *Maggie*.

Another was the *J.J. Loggie*, a 220-ton lumber schooner that was lost in the early morning hours of October 20, 1912, when she went onto the rocks and broke her back about one mile south of Point Arguello. Her crew of eighteen men barely escaped with their lives by rushing from their berths and leaping into the lifeboats. Few had time to dress, and they were suffering severely from exposure when picked up by the steamer *Riverside* at dawn. Outbound from Eureka for San Pedro with 450,000 feet of lumber aboard, the four-year-old ship was lost on a clear, fogless night at the exact spot where the steamer *Santa Rosa* had wrecked a year before.

The years since then have been peppered with losses from enemy action, collision, bad weather and bad judgment. Ironically, the steam schooner *Riverside*, which rescued the crew of the *J.J. Loggie*, was herself wrecked "due to negligence" the following June when she went aground on Blunt's Reef.

Whatever the cause, though, each incident has a story to tell. These are tales of the best and the worst of the human condition—heroism, cowardice, devotion, venality, gallantry, irony and hubris—combined with the unique and sometimes fatal nature of the turbulent and unforgiving waters that endlessly pound California's harsh coastline.

CHAPTER 1

DANGEROUS WATERS

En route to Acapulco from Manila in the fall of 1595, Portuguese explorer Captain Sebastian Rodriguez Cermeno, in command of the galleon *San Agustin*, reached land between Point St. George and Trinidad Head, about 295 miles north of what we now know as San Francisco Bay.

His two-year mission was to explore and map the coast of California, search for suitable anchorages and claim the territory for His Majesty, King Philip II of Spain.

Sailing southward, Cermeno anchored the little galleon off Point Reyes, where she rose and dipped on the gentle swells with a skeleton crew aboard as her captain went ashore with a number of men to plant the flag of Spain and determine if the bay connected to a navigable river.

According to the contemporary record, a violent storm suddenly struck from the southwest without warning and caught the two-hundred-ton *San Agustin* in its grip. Her anchor couldn't hold, and the doomed ship smashed into the treacherous rocks, taking all of the crew on board to their deaths. She was carrying a cargo of silks, spices and porcelain and, contrary to later reports and unlike many of her contemporaries, only a very small amount of gold specie.

Undeterred, Cermeno salvaged a launch from the wreckage, named it the *San Buenaventure* and sailed south, hugging the coast with seventy-nine other men and their provisions and arriving in Acapulco, New Spain, on January 17, 1596.

What's notable is that, in his haste to reach Acapulco, Cermeno sailed his small, overloaded craft right past the mouth of San Francisco Bay, one of the finest natural anchorages in the world, without even noticing.

Three centuries later, in the 1980s and '90s, surveyors from the U.S. National Park Service and the National Oceanic and Atmospheric Administration scanned Drakes Bay for magnetic anomalies that might give up the location of the *San Agustin*, but to date, the wreck has not been located.

THE *BROTHER JONATHAN*: ONLY NINETEEN SURVIVED

The beautiful California Steam Navigation Company side-wheeler *Brother Jonathan* held celebrity status up and down the Pacific Coast, from Panama to British Columbia. Her arrivals and departures were grist for San Francisco newspapers, which followed her career in great detail.

On Sunday, July 30, 1865, seeking shelter from a sudden storm, she struck St. George Reef, about eight miles off Crescent City, with such force that her bottom was torn out. In a matter of minutes, the ship went down in more than one hundred feet of water. Two of the three lifeboats that were

The San Francisco waterfront in the mid-1850s. In the upper center of the image is the ill-fated steamer *Brother Jonathan*. *Courtesy of the San Francisco Maritime NHP.*

launched capsized, throwing their occupants into the raging sea. In the end, only 19 people—5 women, 3 children and 11 crew members—of the 273 aboard the ship survived.

Among the lost were her master, Captain Samuel J. DeWolf; Dr. Anson Henry, Abraham Lincoln's personal physician; Brigadier General George Wright, commanding general of the U.S. Army's Department of the Pacific, and his wife, Margaret; James Nisbit, editor of the *San Francisco Herald*; and Roseanna Keenan, a colorful San Francisco madam who was traveling with seven of her "soiled doves." Also lost were Captain DeWolf's pet Newfoundland dog and, oddly enough, a pair of camels.

The *Brother Jonathan* was also carrying seven hundred tons of miscellaneous freight, including axe handles, doorknobs, crockery, champagne and $50 million in gold. The wreck resulted in the government investing in a lighthouse, although it did not become operational until 1892.

Salvors finally discovered the wreck in 1993, 128 years after she went to the bottom.

THE *WALLA WALLA*: RUN DOWN AND SUNK

Seventy-nine people were drowned and another twenty-nine listed as missing when the coastal steamer *Walla Walla*, captained by "Andy" Hall, was run down and sunk by an unidentified ship off the coast of Mendocino on January 3, 1902.

The culprit vessel did not heave-to to rescue survivors and was never identified, but contemporary sources speculate that she was either the four-masted bark *Europe*, bound from Portland for Cardiff with a cargo of wheat, or the ship *Ernest Legouve*, fifty-five days out from Hobart, Tasmania, for Portland.

Six survivors of the *Walla Walla* were rescued in heavy seas more than thirty-six hours after the ship went down, while several passengers and crew members were commended for their heroism during the incident.

"Don't you dare say a word about me, but give my boys all the credit," Hall told a reporter from the *San Francisco Call*. "There was not a coward in the entire ship's crew. Every man was at his post and not one deserted it. I've lost my ship, but I'm proud of the fact that every man under me was where his duty called him when the shop was in danger."

The day after the wreck, the *San Francisco Call* wrote that one of the missing was the *Walla Walla*'s chief steward, John Connell. The paper noted that he was "one of the oldest employees of the Pacific Coast Steamship Company, his term of service extending over twenty-two years. He was known to thousands who have taken voyages between Pacific Coast ports. He resided at Twelfth and Poplar Streets, Oakland, with his three sisters, who are anxiously awaiting news of him."

The wreck of the *Walla Walla* was Steward Connell's fourth. His first experience was in 1882, when the steamer *Grand Republic* went down off the coast of Oregon, and he was also aboard the steamer *Queen* when she was twice stranded.

Connell's body was never recovered.

The *Corona*: The Master Shoulders the Blame

Battling a fierce wind and a terrific flood tide, Captain Boyd's hopes of safely bringing the steamer *Corona* into Eureka on the morning of March 1, 1907, ended when three great successive seas lifted the 1,492-ton ship onto the Humboldt Bar.

Described as "one of the staunchest vessels on the coast," the *Corona* was sailing for Redondo with ninety-six passengers, 350 tons of miscellaneous cargo and 550 tons of railroad ties for the Southern Pacific Railroad when she was wrecked.

"Either the failure of the quartermaster at the wheel to understand the captain's orders or the inability of the *Corona* to respond to her rudder in the face of the heavy seas that struck her nose in quick succession was responsible for the wreck," wrote the *San Francisco Call*.

Captain Boyd, the *Corona*'s master, shouldered all the blame for the wreck. "I was going full speed ahead until I turned into the channel, then I slackened down. I gave the orders and they were obeyed."

Prior to taking command of the *Corona*, Boyd had served as master of the schooner *Gipsy*, which was lost the previous year at Monterey when a lookout mistook a light marking a sewer maintenance project for a signal indicating her berth.

Most of the *Corona*'s deck cargo of railroad ties floated off and were recovered, and most of the passengers' baggage was salvaged, but the general cargo was waterlogged and deemed beyond saving.

Passengers crowd the upper deck of the doomed steamer *Corona* as crewmen from the Humboldt Bay Life-Saving Station and civilian volunteers struggle to position a lifeboat for a rescue attempt. *Courtesy of the Special Collections Library, Humboldt State University.*

All of her passengers and crew were saved with the exception of Quartermaster Gunn, who drowned when the lifeboat he was put in charge of capsized.

The *La Paz*, the *North Bend* and the *Kingsbury*: Driven Ashore by the "Heaviest Swell"

On December 6, 1855, the *Daily Alta California* published a bulletin from Big River in Mendocino County: "We were visited yesterday by the heaviest swell from the westward that has been experienced on this coast for many years. At the time the swell commenced running, there was laying in this port the Chilian [*sic*] ship *La Paz*, Capt. [illegible], bound for Valparaiso, loading; hermaphrodite brig *North Bend*, Capt. Lent, for San Francisco, loading; the brig *Kingsbury*, O.H. Miller, waiting cargo."

Around noon, the *La Paz* dragged her anchors before she was driven ashore and "broke into a thousand pieces." Acting captain and former first mate Eugene Tablet, his wife, their four-year-old son, the wife of Captain Jules Chazelles and an unnamed sailor died in the wreck.

One hour later, the *North Bend* sprung a severe leak that the pumps were unable to control. Her crew was saved, but the ship was a total loss. At 4:00 p.m., the *Kingsbury* was ground up after she steered into the bluff; her jib boom struck the bank and held just long enough for the men to escape the doomed ship.

Just short of four years later, in April 1859, the *Sacramento Union* lamented that several of the largest lumber mills adjacent to Humboldt Bay were forced to suspend operations because their wharves had been seriously damaged during a particularly bad spate of heavy weather. "The unprecedented loss of vessels on our coast last winter, together with the rapid increase in trade with foreign ports, has produced this effect, and there is the strong probability that this difficulty will exist until a new supply of vessels shall arrive from the other side," the paper wrote.

The paper went on to enumerate the losses—the barks *America* and *Success*, the brigs *Swiss Boy* and *Halcyon* and the schooners *Ryerson* and *Exact*—and added that "all [occurred] within the short space of five months…a heavy blow to lumbermen, and effect[ed], more or less, all branches of trade."

THE *ELLA FLORENCE*, THE *ELSIE IVERSON*, THE *GRACIE BELLE RICHARDSON* AND THE *GOLDEN GATE*: A NAME BY ANY OTHER

Oddly, there are numerous recorded examples of multiple ships bearing the same name being wrecked, sometimes years apart, at the same place on the California coast.

One such example was the brace of schooners bearing the name *Ella Florence* and coming to grief at Kent's Point, Mendocino—one in November 1868 and the other in February 1872.

Three schooners bore the name *Elsie Iverson*. Two were wrecked at Point Arena, one in 1872 and the other in 1886, while the third ended her days eight miles east of the Point Reyes Light in 1888.

Then there was the pair of wooden schooners named the *Gracie Belle Richardson* that plied the California coast in the late 1880s. The exact dates and specific circumstances of their losses are not recorded, but what is known is that both came to grief on the rocky coast of Sonoma County and that their owner, Captain Richardson, swore that he would never use that name on another vessel.

But the record holder in this bizarre category is the name *Golden Gate*. Since 1854, six vessels—three schooners, a pair of sailing ships and a steamer—bearing that name have been wrecked in California waters.

Like Moths to a Flame

The tankers *Lyman Stewart* and *Frank H. Buck* were sisters, built side by side in 1914 at San Francisco's Union Iron Works for separate owners—the *Lyman Stewart* for the Union Oil Company and the *Frank H. Buck* for the Associated Oil Company.

On October 8, 1922, the *Lyman Stewart* drifted onto the rocks at Point Lobos, near the Cliff House, after a collision in a heavy fog with the U.S. flag freighter *Walter Luckenbach*.

Almost fifteen years later, the tanker *Frank H. Buck* sank almost immediately after colliding on March 6, 1937, with the Dollar Steamship Company passenger liner *President Coolidge*—also in a heavy fog at Point Lobos. Both doomed sisters came to rest within yards of each other and within just a few miles of where they were built.

The two-masted lumber schooner *Don Leandro*, stranded at Little River on November 27, 1865, was salvaged and resumed her career hauling lumber along the coast only to go aground at the same location in 1872.

Pulled off again, the schooner reportedly met her end in November 1885 at Little River during what is still considered to be one of the worst storms ever to slam into the coast of Northern California.

Built like her sisters to withstand the usual hazards of their calling, the *California* was an atypical lumber schooner plying her trade along the "Redwood Coast" in the later half of the nineteenth century. She went ashore at Albion in March 1883, suffered only minimal damage and was pulled off to resume her voyage. The following November, she went ashore again at Albion and was again pulled off at high tide with only a few scrapes on her bottom.

The *California*'s routine existence continued for another fourteen years until her end came on May 19, 1897, when she went ashore, this time for good, at…Albion.

THE *CHICO*: "IT WASN'T WHAT IT SEEMED"

Launched in Tacoma as the *Alice Blanchard* in 1890, the little coastal steamer *Chico* went ashore at Shelter Cove, near Eureka, on July 17, 1906, and, over the following weeks, was slowly pounded to kindling.

It was low water at the time of the wreck, and her crew was able to lower themselves over the side and, literally, walk ashore.

According to the *San Francisco Call*, "Captain Martin says he was proceeding along under slow bell in a very heavy fog when suddenly the point at Shelter Cove loomed up. Thinking another vessel was headed for him, he changed his course to avoid a collision and a moment later grounded on the rocks."

A few days after the *Chico* went ashore, the *San Francisco Call* reported that "with her bottom smashed and leaking badly, there is no chance to save the little craft. It is only a question of time until she breaks into bits."

The steamer *Anne Blanchard*, later renamed the *Chico*, became lost in the fog and was wrecked at Shelter Cove. *Author's collection.*

The *Roanoke*: Only Three Survived

Including Captain Richard Dickson and his wife, forty-seven of the fifty people aboard died in the wreck of the steamer *Roanoke* when she capsized off Port San Luis on May 9, 1916, and sank in less than fifteen minutes. The 2,354-ton ship was owned by the North Pacific Steamship Company and had been employed in the coastal passenger trade for many years before she was lost.

The *Roanoke* was bound for Valparaiso with a $250,000 cargo of 600 tons of dynamite, 1,300 tons of wheat and several hundred drums of gasoline and lubricating oil. According to one of the three survivors, Quartermaster Joseph Erbe, the cargo shifted in the mountainous seas and caused the ship to list heavily before she went down.

Among those lost was eighteen-year-old Carlos Belgrano, a senior at Fremont High School in Oakland. The *Sausalito News* reported that the boy's father, vice-president of the Italian Popular Bank, had given him permission to leave school early and sign on as the *Roanoke*'s freight clerk.

Neither Belgrano's body nor those of any of the others lost in the wreck of the *Roanoke* was ever recovered.

The *Howard Olson*: Cut in Half in Excellent Weather

A total of four crewmen were killed when the ten-thousand-ton, C-4-type freighter *Marine Leopard* cut the steel-hulled coastal lumber carrier *Howard Olson* in half like a piece of cake early in the morning of May 14, 1956.

The stern section of the ship sank within three minutes of the collision. The ship's bow section remained floating for several hours before it finally sank, taking three crewmen to the bottom some 2 miles off Point Sur and about 175 miles south of San Francisco.

The *Howard Olson* was outbound from the Port of Los Angeles for Coos Bay, Oregon, to load a cargo of lumber, while the *Marine Leopard* was outbound from San Francisco for the East Coast via the Panama Canal. The cause of the collision remains a mystery, as both weather and visibility were excellent at the time of the collision.

The lumber carrier *Howard Olson* was cut in half in a collision with the freighter *Marine Leopard* off Big Sur on May 14, 1956. *Courtesy of the Historical Collection of the Great Lakes, Bowling Green State University.*

The 2,396-ton *Howard Olson* was built in 1917 at the Great Lakes Engineering Works in Ecorse, Michigan.

THE *CASPAR*: POINT ARENA CLAIMS ANOTHER VICTIM

In her heyday, the *Caspar* was considered one of the best of the "Scandinavian Navy"—a popular nickname of the period that acknowledged the disproportionate number of Swedes, Danes and Norwegians who officered and crewed many of the scores of small ships that carried lumber, passengers and cargo up and down the West Coast.

Built in 1888 by Hansen & Frazer in San Francisco, the steam schooner could carry as much as 340,000 board feet of lumber at a time—enough to build twenty small houses—both on deck and in her hold.

Her nine years of yeoman's service for the Caspar Lumber Company ended near Point Arena when she was driven off course, piled onto Saunders Reef and capsized on October 22, 1897.

Of the *Caspar*'s crew of fifteen, only two survived: her master, Captain Olaf Anfindsen, and a seaman named Chris Larsen. Only one body was recovered—that of George Offerman, the *Caspar*'s chief engineer, which washed ashore about a mile north of the wreck.

A number of ships had been lost at Point Arena in the years before the *Caspar* was wrecked. They included the steamer *San Benito*, wrecked a year previously at the same spot with a loss of six of her crew.

THE *RHODERICK DHU*: A SAILING TANKER AGROUND AND LOST

Named for a character in Sir Walter Scott's poem "The Lady of the Lake," the *Rhoderick Dhu* was built in 1874 in Sutherland, England, for the Australia trade. Acquired by the Matson Navigation Company in 1901 to serve on the route between San Francisco and Honolulu, the three-masted bark was the first sailing ship to be equipped with both electric lights and a cold-storage plant. The 257-foot-long ship was sold to the Associated Oil Company in 1906 and converted into a tanker. She went aground on the rocks at Point Pinos near the entrance to Monterey Bay on April 26, 1909, and was lost.

According to the wreck report, the tugs *Relief* and *Defiance* later attempted to take her in tow but only caused the ship to list to seaward, her holds filling

The three-masted square-rigger *Rhoderick Dhu* before her conversion to a sailing tanker in 1906. She was wrecked just three years later. *Courtesy of the Pacific Grove Museum of Natural History.*

with water. Later, a hole was cut in her hull, and her donkey engine, pumps, masts, spars and rigging were salvaged.

THE USS *F-1*: ON ETERNAL PATROL

The U.S. Navy submarine USS *F-1* sank in deep water off La Jolla, near San Diego, on December 17, 1917, after colliding with a sister ship, the submarine USS *F-3*.

With her port side torn from the engine room to the bow, the *F-1* sank within ten seconds, taking nineteen sailors with her more than 635 feet to the bottom. Her commanding officer, Lieutenant Alfred Montgomery, and four enlisted men survived and were picked out of the water by the *F-3* and brought to San Pedro.

Earlier in her career, the boat had, for a time, held the world deep-dive record of 283 feet.

The sub still rests on the bottom, located in October 1975 by a U.S. Navy oceanographic research ship using side-scan sonar while conducting a routine search for a Navy F-4J Phantom jet that had ditched in the sea off Point Loma. According to the official report published after the wreck was discovered, "The boat is lying on its starboard side with the hole made by *F-3* clearly visible. The hull is in amazingly good shape and serves as a deep grave site for the U.S. Naval Submarine Force's first wartime submarine loss."

THE *WINFIELD SCOTT*: TRAGICALLY SHORT-LIVED

The popular passenger steamer *Winfield Scott*, launched in New York in 1851, was hailed for her remarkable speed and handsome fittings, but her career under the Pacific Mail Steamship Company house flag was destined to be tragically short-lived.

One of the most highly regarded ships employed on the so-called Isthmian route between San Francisco and Panama, the wooden side-wheeler boasted fully lighted and ventilated $350-per-voyage staterooms

Named for the hero of the Mexican War, the *Winfield Scott* was considered to be one of the most handsome ships serving the Panama–San Francisco route. *Courtesy of the San Francisco Maritime NHP.*

for her 165 first-class passengers, comfortable accommodations for 150 steerage passengers and a ninety-six-foot-long dining room that could seat 100 people at a time.

Her all-too-brief career ended on December 1, 1853, when she was wrecked on a rock outcropping off the fog-blanketed eastern shore of Anacapa Island, one of seven rocky Channel Islands clustered off the coast of Southern California.

The *Winfield Scott* had been acquired by the PMSC to replace the *Tennessee*, which had been lost just nine months previously.

THE *LOUIS*:
A "REMARKABLY UNATTRACTIVE" SCHOONER

Outbound from Grays Harbor, Washington, with a load of 900,000 feet of railroad ties for the Southern Pacific Company in San Francisco, the schooner *Louis* piled onto fog-shrouded South Farallon Island on June 19, 1907.

A distress signal summoned a steam tug, which transported the Fort Point and Point Bonita Life-Saving Service crews to the site, where they rigged a breeches buoy and were able to lift five members of the crew to safety. The five remaining members of the schooner's crew made it to safety in the ship's lifeboat.

The first of her rig to sail around the world, the five-masted *Louis* was originally constructed as a steamer, and according to maritime historian Gordon Newell, her conversion to sail resulted in her being turned into "a remarkably unattractive vessel…some of her masts being stepped out of alignment on each side of the keelson."

Over the years, he wrote, her homely appearance didn't improve, as "she was so badly hogged that it was said her decks were washed down from amidships so that the water could run off at both ends."

THE *NORLINA*: WRECKED AS THE
CAPTAIN SLEEPS ONE OFF

Aground on the rocks off Salt Point about forty-five miles north of San Francisco, the *Norlina* became a total loss while steaming northbound from the Golden Gate to Seattle via Portland with a general cargo on August 4, 1926.

Her master, Captain John Soderlun, had retired for the night at ten o'clock and had left Second Mate Fred Atwood in charge on the bridge. Several hours later, a thick fog dropped like a blanket on the ship, and several attempts to wake Soderlun failed. Atwood reduced the ship's speed by half, but it was too late.

The impact roused the somnolent captain, who immediately sent out an SOS with an incorrect position. A tug and a U.S. Coast Guard cutter were dispatched to the reported position and found the wrecked ship three miles away after a search of several hours in the fog.

The steamer *Norlina* aground off Salt Point, just north of the Golden Gate, August 26, 1926. *Author's collection.*

Two months after the wreck, a salvage company's attempt to pull the *Norlina* off the rocks failed when a sudden gale erupted and the ship broke in half after crashing into another reef nearby. Driven ashore for the last time, she was salvaged where she lay and her hull finally dynamited.

The 4,596-ton freighter had been built in West Hartlepool, England, in 1909 as the *Harfleur*. She was transferred to American registry and renamed *Georgiana* in 1915. The following year, she was purchased by American owners and renamed *Norlina*.

Acquired in 1917 for service as a U.S. Navy transport, she was decommissioned in May 1919 and delivered to the U.S. Shipping Board for simultaneous return to her owner, the Garland Steamship Company of New York City.

An official investigation determined that the captain, as well as both the second and third mates, were, "in all probability," drunk at the time of the wreck.

THE *OHIOAN*: ON THE ROCKS SHE REMAINED

The freighter *Ohioan* was one of eight sister ships built in 1914 by the Maryland Steel Company for the American-Hawaiian Steamship Company's U.S.

A sizable crowd of curious onlookers view the American-Hawaiian Steamship Company freighter *Ohioan*, impaled on the rocks near San Francisco's Cliff House. *Author's collection.*

intercoastal service that connected ports along the U.S. East, Gulf and West Coasts via the Panama Canal.

She sailed as a U.S. Navy transport during World War I and returned to merchant service in 1919. The ship was lost early in the morning hours of October 7, 1936, when she ran aground at Point Lobos, just south of the Golden Gate. Her cargo included case oil and explosives.

A pair of U.S. Coast Guard surfboats took thirty-one crewmen off the ship, and several efforts over the next few weeks to salvage the ship failed.

The *Ohioan* and her cargo were finally sold for $2,800. The ship remained on the rocks and finally broke in two during a fierce December 1937 storm that also sank the *Ellen F.*, a salvage ship that was working on the wrecked freighter.

The USCGC *McCulloch*: The *"Mac"* Comes to Grief

The *McCulloch* was built in Philadelphia, Pennsylvania. She was commissioned into the U.S. Revenue Cutter Service (forerunner of the U.S. Coast Guard) in December 1897 and soon thereafter steamed eastward, bound for the Pacific via the Suez Canal.

When she arrived in Asiatic waters, the threat of war with Spain caused the *McCulloch* to be reassigned to service with the navy. She was commended for her participation in the Manila campaign during the Spanish-American War and, upon her return to the U.S. Treasury Department, was assigned to patrol the waters from Alaska to Mexico.

Over the years, the "*Mac*," as she was known, became a fixture on the Pacific Coast, participating in many humanitarian and law enforcement missions. She was commended for aiding in the relief efforts following the San Francisco earthquake of 1906, as well as conducting rescue and salvage operations involving numerous shipwrecks.

Again transferred to navy control during World War I, the *McCulloch* sank on June 13, 1917, three miles northwest of Point Conception, after colliding with the Pacific Steamship Company steamer *Governor*. None of her crew was lost in the collision.

THE *EMIDIO*, THE *MONTEBELLO* AND THE *LARRY DOHENY*: THREE VICTIMS OF WAR

The General Petroleum Corp. tanker *Emidio* bore the dubious distinction of becoming the first casualty of the Imperial Japanese Navy's submarine campaign along the California coastline.

On December 20, 1941, less than two weeks after the attack on Pearl Harbor, the 6,912-ton ship was sailing in ballast from Seattle to San Pedro when she was abandoned off Cape Mendocino after being shelled by the Japanese submarine *I-17*. Five members of her crew were killed while trying to launch one of the ship's lifeboats.

The abandoned ship drifted eighty-five miles northward and went on the rocks near Crescent City, where she broke up. The thirty-one survivors rowed the remaining three lifeboats for sixteen hours through a driving rainstorm until they were picked up by a U.S. Coast Guard lightship a few miles off Humboldt Bay.

Three days later, the 8,272-ton steam tanker *Montebello* played cat-and-mouse with the Japanese submarine *I-21*, which repeatedly shelled the tanker and finally sent her to the bottom with a single torpedo just six miles off

Just two weeks after Pearl Harbor, the Union Oil tanker *Montebello* was sunk by a Japanese submarine off the California coast. *Courtesy of the Vancouver Maritime Museum.*

Cambria. The tanker, owned by the Union Oil Company of California, was bound for Vancouver, British Columbia, with more than three million gallons of crude oil in her tanks. All thirty-eight crewmen escaped in four lifeboats and survived despite being machine-gunned by the crew of the *I-21*.

Seventy years later, a federal and state multi-agency expedition launched a $2.3 million effort to test whether the oil was still aboard the sunken tanker, which rests nine hundred feet below the surface, just south of the Monterey Bay National Marine Sanctuary. After an exhaustive eleven-day examination of the wreck, it was found that there was no environmental danger of the ship's eighteen cargo tanks leaking because they were found to be completely empty.

On October 26, 1942, several miles southwest of Eureka, the Richfield Oil Company tanker *Larry Doheny* was torpedoed and sunk by the Japanese submarine *I-2*. Two crewmen and four U.S. Navy armed guards were killed in the sinking, with a navy "Q Ship," the USS *Anacapa*, rescuing the tanker's thirty-eight survivors.

The previous December, the tanker had been shelled by the Japanese submarine *I-17*, the same sub that sank the tanker *Emidio*, but escaped with moderate damage.

THE *BENEVOLENCE*: GONE IN FIFTEEN MINUTES

On August 25, 1950, the U.S. Navy hospital ship *Benevolence* collided with the freighter *Mary Luckenbach* in heavy fog off the Golden Gate and sank in just fifteen minutes. More than five hundred members of her crew were rescued, while twenty-three lost their lives with the ship coming to rest on her port side in seventy-five feet of water.

U.S. Navy captain T.R. Wirth, chief of staff of the Twelfth Naval District in San Francisco, wrote later that the *Benevolence* keeled over within fifteen minutes after the collision. "Thank God the ship wasn't returning from Korea. Normally, there would have been fifteen hundred patients aboard, maybe even as many as three thousand," he later told the *San Francisco Chronicle*.

The ship was launched in 1944 as the C-4-type freighter *Marine Lion*. She was converted shortly thereafter into an 802-bed hospital ship, renamed and was present in Tokyo Bay at the signing of the Japanese surrender in September 1945.

The *Benevolence* was decommissioned and placed in strategic reserve in 1947. She was returning from her sea trials prior to her assignment to the Military Sea Transportation Service when the fatal collision occurred.

With one of her Red Cross hull markings still visible, this eerie image of the U.S. Navy hospital ship *Benevolence* was taken just moments after she rolled over onto her port side and went to the bottom of San Francisco Bay. *Courtesy of the U.S. Naval History & Heritage Command Center.*

The ship's white hull marked with large red crosses was clearly visible at low water and was deemed a hazard to navigation by the U.S. Coast Guard. The wreck was later dynamited after salvage was deemed impractical.

THE *RHINE MARU*: HOPES DASHED AT BIG SUR

A light and a resonant horn weren't enough to keep the fog-shrouded Japanese freighter *Rhine Maru* from being impaled on a reef off Big Sur River on March 28, 1930.

Bound from San Francisco to San Pedro with a cargo of baled cotton, machinery, borax and gypsum, the 6,577-ton ship was lost just three miles from the Big Sur Lighthouse and fog signal.

Soon after the ship went aground, her crew was taken aboard the steamer *Humboldt*, which had responded immediately to the *Rhine Maru*'s distress call.

An initial salvage survey was optimistic that both the ship and her cargo could be saved, and her owners—Tokyo-headquartered Kawasaki Kaisen Kaisha— hired the firm of Merritt, Chapman & Scott to head the salvage operation.

Within a few weeks, two-thirds of the *Rhine Maru*'s cargo had been taken off, but increasingly ugly weather eventually ended the salvage effort with the ship going to pieces in mountainous, storm-lashed waves.

The Japanese-flag freighter *Rhine Maru* was lost in the fog off Big Sur. *Courtesy of the San Francisco Maritime NHP.*

The *Isabelita Heyne*: A "Very Fast Sailer" Disappears

Built in Philadelphia in 1848, the clipper bark *Isabelita Heyne* was a "staunch" workhorse in the California–China trade, but her career as a "very fast sailer" came to an abrupt end on January 1, 1856, when, inbound from Hong Kong, she went ashore about thirty-five miles south of Half Moon Bay.

The ship sat on the beach for days with her master and first mate aboard. Both had refused to leave the ship, and a minor mystery developed when it seemed to literally vanish along with the two men. According to the *Sacramento Daily Union*, "She had either gone to pieces or filled and sunk, there being about four or five fathoms of water at the point where she was last seen…the captain and first mate were doubtless drowned."

Rumors, all of which proved to be unfounded, circulated along the waterfront of the ship being run aground to cover evidence of a mutiny by the crew; her cargo of rice, tea and sugar disappearing; and the decapitated body of the captain seen lashed to her mainmast shrouds.

The last mention of the ship in the local press is a brief in the *Daily Alta California* of February 10 stating that "the wreck of the *Isabelita Heyne* has all disappeared, all burnt up by the wreckers on the beach."

It's worth noting that two years before her loss, the ship was lauded for making the run from Hong Kong to San Francisco in just forty-one days, one of the fastest voyages under sail ever made between the two ports.

The *Chickasaw*: On the Rocks in the Fog

The American-flag freighter *Chickasaw* was lost when she went aground on February 7, 1962, in a thick fog on Santa Rosa Island off the coast of Southern California.

A C-2-type cargo transport, she was built in 1942 and served as a U.S. Navy transport, the USS *Thurston*, until 1946. She saw extensive service in World War II in both the European and Pacific Theaters, landing troops, equipment and supplies at Normandy, Iwo Jima and Okinawa and conducting several other amphibious operations. Two years after the war ended, she was sold

The Waterman Steamship Company freighter *Chickasaw*, aground and wrecked on Santa Rosa Island, February 1962. *Courtesy of Robert V. Schwemmer.*

to the Waterman Steamship Company of Mobile, Alabama, demilitarized and renamed *Chickasaw*.

She was outbound from Yokohama, Japan, for the Port of Los Angeles with a $1.5 million cargo of general merchandise that included plywood, shoes, toys, dishes and a 1950s-vintage Buick. Most of the cargo was salvaged by shuttling Conex boxes carried on the ship to the bluff overlooking the wreck via a cable system that resembled a high-wire trapeze.

What remains of the 439-foot-long, 5,185-ton *Chickasaw* still lay where she went aground, rusting away. For years, her stack, still bearing the Waterman livery, acted as her grave marker.

CHAPTER 2

"EQUAL TO HIS DUTY"

The span of the entire nineteenth century saw tremendous developments in maritime technology as Maine-built "Down Easters" and sleek clippers from Boston and New York yards challenged Cape Horn with thousands of California-bound passengers aboard, while steam-powered side-wheelers of iron and steel slowly and cautiously gained prominence.

Over time, wood gave way to iron and steel, and sail gave way to steam—but not without a price. As in every era, leaps in infant technologies often led to tragic disasters that brought out the best—and, sometimes, the worst—in the characters involved in them. One of those who proved to be "more than equal to his duty" was Captain J.C. Bogart of the veteran side-wheeler *Sierra Nevada*.

Bogart took to his cabin on the evening of October 17, 1869, confident that his ship was safely on course, plodding down the coast at six and a half knots through the fog, en route from San Francisco to San Luis Obispo via Santa Cruz and Monterey.

Soundings had been taken, charts had been checked and all was well. Retiring to his cabin, only twenty minutes passed before his chief officer burst through the door to announce that breakers were dead ahead. Sprinting to the bridge, Bogart ordered the helm "hard a port" just as the ship went onto a reef three miles north of Pedro Blanco.

The engine was ordered "full astern" just as a massive swell carried the ship farther onto the reef, keeling her over and sealing her fate, with her stack toppled over and water rapidly filling her hold and engine room.

The side-wheeler *Sierra Nevada* wrecked on October 17, 1869. *Author's collection.*

As Bogart, later called "more than equal to his duty," and his officers and crew assisted passengers into four lifeboats, an incident occurred that brought Bogart to tears when he later recounted it in an interview with the *Daily Alta California*.

Among those aboard the *Sierra Nevada* were Illinois governor John Wood and his wife, two sons and a brother-in-law. Ordered into one of the lifeboats, Wood replied, "No. Nearly all here are young men to whom life is of value. I am 74 years of age. I will wait."

Wood did bravely wait his turn and, like the other seventy-seven passengers and crew aboard, was eventually saved after spending the night in his lifeboat and finally making landfall near San Simeon the following morning.

The *Sierra Nevada*, though, did not survive, as both she and her cargo of unspecified "merchandise" were a total loss.

The "elegant" ship had been launched in 1851 as the *Texas* and was first employed on the route between New York and Chagres, Panama, before sailing for the West Coast, where she later set a record of seventy-two hours for the run from the Golden Gate to Portland.

The *Independence*: A Hero Immortalized

A ship—and loss—typical of the period of California's madcap rush onto the world stage was the steamer *Independence*, operated by Cornelius Vanderbilt's Independent Line.

On October 16, 1853, the steamer was bound for San Francisco from San Juan del Sur, Nicaragua, and Acapulco, Mexico, when she struck a reef off the coast of Baja California, caught fire and sank about three hundred yards from shore.

Estimates of the number of people lost in the wreck range from 130 to 175 passengers and crewmen, with the tragedy making headlines from San Francisco to London.

The hero of the day was one of the ship's engineers, later credited with saving the lives of more than ninety men, women and children when the *Independence* was lost. Giving up the seafaring life, he later joined the predecessor of the San Francisco Fire Department and would, years later, become a close personal friend and poker partner of the young Mark Twain, who later memorialized his companion in his first novel.

The former *Independence* engineer's name was Tom Sawyer.

The *Bear*: A Case of "Contributory Negligence"

For six years, the passenger steamer *Bear* had plied the route between Portland and San Francisco for the San Francisco & Portland Steamship Company.

On the late evening of June 14, 1916, the 4,500-ton ship was headed southbound, carefully feeling her way through the thick fog that blanketed the Mendocino coastline with 182 passengers and crew aboard. Relying on soundings and charts that convinced him that the *Bear* was at least three miles offshore and well clear of a maze of treacherous reefs, Captain Louis Nopander altered course for Point Arena. Instead, within the hour, the ship had stranded fast on a reef about one hundred yards off Cape Mendocino.

"Abandon ship!" was sounded, with twenty-nine passengers taking to a lifeboat in an attempt to reach shore. The boat capsized almost immediately after it was launched, with five of those aboard drowning in the crashing

With black smoke pouring from her stack, the coastal steamer *Bear* heads out from San Francisco for Portland, Oregon, circa 1916. *Courtesy of the Golden Gate NRA.*

surf. Locals collected the survivors who made it to shore and took them to nearby Capetown, where they were given shelter at the Country Hotel.

About 150 of the remaining passengers and crew elected to row out to the Blunts Reef Lightship rather than try to beach their boat in the crashing breakers. Crowded aboard the lightship but safe, they were transferred the following morning to the passing steamer *Grace Dollar*, which carried the survivors to Eureka.

Charges of incompetence, negligence and even complicity to intentionally wreck the ship flew back and forth in the weeks following the wreck, but after a lengthy investigation, the loss of the ship was blamed on faulty charts and what was deemed "contributory negligence" on the part of Captain Nopander and his officers.

Several hundred tons of rolled newsprint valued at $50,000 were salvaged and moved from the vessel to the beach. The paper was purchased by Arthur M. Smith, publisher of the local *Humboldt Times* newspaper. Also recovered were cases of condensed milk, several hundred sacks of flour and the body of a $7,000 Thoroughbred horse that drowned during an attempt to pull it out of the stranded ship's hold.

Several attempts to refloat the *Bear*, valued at $1 million, failed, and she broke up. But her engine room equipment and boilers were salvaged and later sold in Eureka.

The *City of Chester*: "Heartrending Scenes"

For years, the Pacific Coast Steamship Company's *City of Chester* had served the lumber ports—both large and small—that dotted the Humboldt coast with cargo and passenger service.

A "fine, staunch" vessel, the little steamer was outbound from San Francisco for Eureka on the foggy morning of August 22, 1888, when she was rammed in mid-channel off Fort Point by the 420-foot-long, British-flag passenger liner *Oceanic*.

Pandemonium reigned, and "heartrending scenes were witnessed by the survivors" as she went to the bottom, taking twenty-four passengers and crewmen with her.

In the days following the disaster, recriminations flew back and forth as the masters of both ships said they gave the proper signals to avoid the collision, and the ship's crew was alternately accused by some of cowardice and incompetence and lauded by still others as heroes.

But there was agreement on all sides regarding the heroic conduct of one particular crewman aboard the *Oceanic*, which drew praise and a commendation from the Court of Inquiry called to investigate the loss of the *City of Chester*. He had unhesitatingly dived from the liner's deck into the debris-filled water to save a struggling two-year-old boy from drowning.

The seaman's name was Ah Lung, and for a Chinese man to be given any credit at all for anything whatsoever was highly unusual at a time when, sadly, strong anti-Chinese sentiment infected not only California but the rest of the country as well.

A letter to the *San Francisco Chronicle* succinctly framed the sentiment: "In connection with our recent steamship disaster…I refer to the bravery of the Chinaman who rescued the little boy from drowning at the imminent risk of his own life. We are not at all partial to the Chinese and have not a very high opinion of their courage, yet such an act is the one unnoticed and is worthy of our recognition…Honor to whom honor is due."

The *Brignardello*: The Master "Didn't Know Where He Was"

On September 3, 1868, outbound from Valparaiso for San Francisco with a cargo of marble blocks, walnuts and olive oil, the Italian-flag *Brignardello* went aground about a quarter mile south of the Cliff House.

The *Daily Alta California* wrote that the bark "ran square head on shore, and the surf rolls in on either side without giving her the least list to port or starboard. At the stern, she is about eight feet in the sand and four feet at the bows." The ship "stands up as square as if alongside of the dock, and from the beach looks to the landsman's eye as if 'all right,' but to the sailor she is in a tight place, from which she may never be moved."

A week after the wreck, gangway on trestlework was constructed from the beach to the bows of the stranded bark, allowing a small party of stevedores to salvage some of the ship's cargo from her flooded hold.

The loss of the *Brignardello* was later blamed on poor navigation as the bark's captain "thought he was 40 miles out to sea, not having taken an observation for five days, and consequently not knowing where he was," reported the paper.

The *Alaska*: A Captain Goes Down with His Ship

On August 6, 1921, 38 people died when the coastal passenger steamer *Alaska*, captained by Harold Hobey, stranded on Blunts Reef off Humboldt. She was carrying 131 passengers and a crew of 80. Inbound to San Francisco from Portland via Astoria, she went onto the reef in a dense fog, listed to starboard and sank within fifteen minutes.

The ship's SOS attracted the James Griffiths Co. steamer *Anyox*, which immediately responded to the distress call and was responsible for the rescue of 96 passengers and 70 crew members.

The *Alaska* was built in 1889 as the *Kansas City*. Acquired by the Alaska Steamship Co. in 1915, the ship was chartered to the San Francisco–Portland Steamship Co. when she was lost.

After an investigation and "careful consideration" of the evidence, the U.S. Steamboat Inspection Service filed its report, which stated, "It is positively

The veteran coastal steamer *Alaska* was built in 1889 and went to the bottom in 1921. *Author's collection.*

shown that Capt. Hobey was responsible for the loss of the steamer *Alaska* through his negligence in navigating his vessel at full speed in a dense fog without taking soundings." Calling it a "painful duty," the board laid the responsibility on the captain, "who was in charge of the vessel when she took the rocks, for not slowing or stopping, or using the lead, as it was his duty to do."

Captain Hobey was not on hand to receive the judgment in person. With the *Alaska* sinking beneath him, he refused to board a lifeboat or even don a life jacket and went down with his ship.

The *Yankee Blade*: Craven Coward or Gallant Hero?

Sailing for the Independent Line, the year-old side-wheeler *Yankee Blade* sailed from San Francisco for Panama with a crew of 120 and 800 passengers and a shipment of gold estimated to be worth as much as $213,000 or more.

At 3:30 p.m. on Sunday, October 1, 1854, the ship, under the command of Captain Henry Randall, was running at top speed through a heavy fog when she slammed into the rocks off Point Conception, with about a mile of rough water separating the stranded ship from the almost invisible coast of Santa Barbara County.

An attempt to pull the 1,767-ton, 274-foot-long ship off the reef by reversing her engines failed, leaving a gash 1 foot wide and 30 feet long in her hull. Water poured into the ship, and it became quickly apparent that she was doomed.

Breathless stories of confusion, thievery and murder by malefactors who'd boarded the ship in San Francisco "armed with pistols and Bowie knives" appeared in the press.

The conduct of Captain Randall after the wreck was the subject of several newspaper stories—florid examples of journalistic excess that, on the one hand, accused him of "craven cowardice" for not staying aboard the stricken *Yankee Blade* and, on the other, praised him for leaving the wreck to carry women and children ashore and making the return trip to the doomed ship several times to repeat the exhausting process.

"How Capt. Randall could have acted better, more actively, or contributed more to the rescue of the passengers, we must confess ourselves at a loss to imagine," opined the *Daily Alta California*. A survivor, J.B. Goddard, wrote in the same edition of the paper: "I feel that Capt. Randall did all he could, or that could be expected of him or any man on the occasion, and the calamity is severe enough on him without the addition of unfounded aspersions from men not accustomed to a ship and the emergencies of a wreck."

But the bravery Captain Randall displayed following the wreck couldn't absolve him of racing through the fog at full speed with a recklessness that destroyed his ship and cost the lives of a still undetermined number of people. To add insult to injury, it was alleged that Randall was in a race with the steamer *Sonoma*—a race on which he'd placed a $5,000 bet.

The unvarnished wrath of the survivors of the wreck was made public with a "resolution" that appeared a few days after the wreck in the *Daily Alta California*. The document was drawn up at a meeting of the survivors in San Francisco's Portsmouth Square and condemned not only Captain Randall but also "the managers of the *Yankee Blade* in directing her course and in running so near a coast well known to be dangerous" and "not forwarding to New York the passengers of the *Yankee Blade* in conformity with their tickets, but leaving them to the charity of the citizens of San Francisco without the means to buy a meal or victuals or a night's lodging."

The survivors also elected to "make a collection among the charitably disposed, the proceeds to be handed over to the Third Mate of the *Yankee Blade* [William Quinn], as a tribute of the esteem for his gallant conduct during the late unfortunate shipwreck, he being left entirely destitute."

According to one newspaper account, "During the proceedings, the agents of the line fearing violence sent to the police office and requested the Marshal to send down five or six police officers to prevent any outrage."

A few days after the resolution was published, the paper printed a letter from one of the survivors thanking Mr. Alden, "the gentlemanly proprietor of Alden's Restaurant, Long Wharf, for his kindness in supplying us with food and drink free of charge."

The *Sarah*: A Good Ship Dishonored

The tale told of the schooner *Sarah*, reported lost on July 26, 1867, was heart wrenching—at least at first. Struck by a heavy swell, she capsized and was cast ashore about fifteen miles north of Santa Cruz, according to her master, Captain Swann, with two of his crew—seamen Jeremiah Trask and Frank Scott—tragically washed overboard and drowned while the remainder of the crew made it ashore to safety.

But something was amiss. On August 8, the *Sacramento Union* reported, "There is some mystery about the loss of the schooner *Sarah*, capsized off Santa Cruz two weeks since. She had on board $32,000 worth of spirits, and cleared for Amoor [*sic*] River, for which insurance is claimed. It has transpired that she had been two weeks at Baker's Bay before meeting the mishap south of this port. The agent sent down by the underwriters had the wreck pumped out, but cannot find a single package of spirits, and none have come ashore."

Three days later, the *Daily Alta California* ran a story under the following breathless running headline: "Bold Attempt at Fraud upon the Customs and Insurance Companies—Arrest of the Captain and Crew—Discovery and Seizure of a Part of the Cargo—The Goods Found in a Cave near Point Reyes—The Captain Denies All Knowledge of the Hiding—The Report of Sailors Drowned Discredited—And the Vessel Is Thought to Have Been Injured Purposely."

Captain Swann, his first and second mates and the ship's cook were arrested and jailed, and it was soon revealed that the luckless sailors Jeremiah Trask and Frank Scott had never existed in the first place and that the story surrounding the loss of the *Sarah* was nothing less than an elaborate insurance scam.

The entire episode, the *Daily Alta California* wrote, was "the most singular, open-handed, bold, and at the same time, clumsy attempt to swindle and defraud the owners, Customs and underwriters out of a large sum, which has come to our knowledge in many a day."

The *Ventura*: A Thick Fog, a Faulty Compass and a Drunken Master

Launched in 1866 as a third-class screw steamer, the USS *Resaca* was assigned to the U.S. Navy's Pacific Squadron patrolling the North American coast from Panama to Alaska and showing the flag on cruises to New Zealand, Tahiti and Valparaiso. She was decommissioned in 1873 and sold for $41,000 to a trio of San Francisco businessmen who had her rebuilt as a passenger-cargo steamer. Her masts removed and renamed the *Ventura*, the 775-ton ship was operated by the Goodall, Nelson & Perkins Steamship Co. in service along the California coast.

She was carrying 186 passengers, all of whom survived, and a cargo of linen, pre-fabricated wagons and general merchandise southbound from San Francisco when she went hard aground near Monterey at 9:00 p.m. on April 20, 1875.

The official wreck report read, "A thick fog and compasses faulty. Captain Fake was reported drunk at the time the Ventura stranded on the outcropping of rocks, two miles north of Point Sur. After the stranding, eleven of the crew left in two of the lifeboats, and were not seen until the next day."

The *Polynesia*: A Mutinous Crew's Revenge

On March 3, 1862, several deserters from the iron clipper *Polynesia*, anchored in San Francisco Bay, slipped ashore in one of the ship's boats.

The "first class" extreme clipper *Polynesia. Courtesy of the San Francisco Maritime NHP.*

Apprehended almost immediately by the San Francisco Police, they were returned aboard.

Later that same day, the disgruntled crewmen reportedly set a fire that destroyed the 1,084-ton ship while she was "lying in the steam abreast of the Market Street Wharf, and ready to sail yesterday morning for Honolulu and Hong Kong, whither she was bound in ballast," according to the *Daily Alta California*.

All efforts to save the ship failed, and when the fire finally burned out, all that was left of the ship was her hull. The would-be deserters were arrested and charged with setting the ship afire, put in irons and held at the Station House.

In addition to her merchandise cargo, lost in the arson fire were a dozen bags of registered mail for Honolulu and China. Originally valued at $50,000, what was left of the *Polynesia* was later sold at auction for $2,300 cash.

THE *HELEN W. ALMY*:
AN UNSEAWORTHY "COFFIN SHIP"

The question of why the *Helen W. Almy* was lost on the stormy night of March 20, 1898, will never be known.

Outward bound from San Francisco for the Alaska gold fields with forty would-be miners and crew, the three-masted bark capsized and went to the bottom with all aboard somewhere between Point Reyes and the South Farallons.

Just three weeks before the wreck, the ship had been purchased by a syndicate of Bay Area businessmen for use in the Alaska trades. The day of the disaster, the ship's new owners ordered the *Almy* to sail despite the misgivings of her master, Captain Hogan, who expressed concern over the gathering storm.

Five days after the wreck, the *Los Angeles Herald* angrily opined, "There have been several wrecks and considerable loss of life arising from the conditions since the rush to the Klondike began, but the most aggravated case has been that of the *Helen W. Almy*, which was wrecked last Monday in plain sight of the port it sailed from—San Francisco. The vessel is a total wreck, not worth salvage, and all on board, forty in number, are supposed to have been lost."

The *Almy*, the paper fumed, "was a coffin ship. She was launched in 1859, and long ago was condemned as unseaworthy. No marine company would insure her. Her timbers were scandalously rotten; in short, her condition was a by-word among sailors. Yet, she was good enough for the Alaskan trade. The great rush to Alaska has not yet begun." The doomed ship, the newspaper concluded, "is not the only Alaskan-bound ship that will touch the bottom of the ocean. Men who are inflamed with the greed for gold will listen to no words of caution. Is there nothing that can be done to prevent further murder and suicide? Is there no law that will reach the men who send such ships to sea?"

THE *RIVERSIDE*: "NEGLIGENCE AND UNSKILLFULNESS"

A lumber carrier sailing for the Charles Nelson Company, the *Riverside* grounded near Blunts Reef and was wrecked on June 19, 1913.

An investigation was held into her loss, and her master, Captain John Dahlquist, had his license suspended for three months. He was found guilty of negligence for leaving the *Riverside*'s bridge in charge of the third mate, Carl A. Lundquist, "without leaving instructions that he should be notified when the Blunts Reef Lightship was sighted so a change of course could be ordered." Lundquist lost his license for a year after being found guilty of "negligence and unskillfulness."

According to the *San Francisco Call*, "It is reported that the loss of the steamer *Riverside*…will considerably delay lumber shipments from this port. The lumber carriers are busy, and the loss of the *Riverside*, together with that of the *Charles Nelson*, burned several months ago, will mean more or less delay."

The *Pomona*: Ashore and Safe "without Even Getting Their Feet Wet"

The Pacific Coast Steamship Co. steamer *Pomona* was some eighteen miles off course outbound from San Francisco for Eureka when she came to grief on March 18, 1908, on the rocks near Fort Ross.

The *Pomona*, her funnel gone and listing to starboard, goes down by the stern as the steamer *Greenwood* stands by after several attempts to tow the stricken ship to safety failed. *Courtesy of the San Francisco Maritime NHP.*

Her passengers reached the shore and safety "without even getting their feet wet," according to the *San Francisco Call*, which added that, "As a shipwreck, the loss of the *Pomona* was in a class by itself."

Most of the passengers were seasick when the ship struck the first rock, the paper wrote. "In the gentle excitement that followed the 'mal de mer' vanished and the sudden subsiding of the inward disturbance more than compensated for the slight inconvenience that followed."

The wreck was dynamited as a navigational hazard several months later after an extensive salvage operation was completed.

The *Pomona*'s first mate and other officers were absolved of all responsibility for the wreck, but her master, Captain Charles Swanson, had his license suspended for six months after a government inquiry into the wreck found him "unskillful in navigating his vessel so close to the shore and in deviating from the usual course."

To his credit, it was noted that Captain Swanson had stated repeatedly during the investigation that he, and he alone, was responsible for the loss of his ship.

THE *R.D. INMAN*: A JONAH ABOARD

The 186-foot-long steam schooner *R.D. Inman* was sailing from San Francisco for Portland, in ballast, when she ran onto the rocks near Bolinas during a severe electrical storm on March 20, 1909.

The *Los Angeles Times* reported that her captain, mistaking a brushfire onshore for another ship on fire, altered course to come to the phantom vessel's aid, only to impale his command on the rugged shoreline.

Her keel snapped, the ship, owned and operated by the Loop Lumber Company and valued at $100,000, was a total loss and was soon reduced to kindling in the breakers.

According to the *San Francisco Call*, one of the survivors of the wreck was seaman John Helander, who "acknowledges himself a Jonah to the extent of three wrecks. He was cast away in the brigantine *Nanne* some years ago and was a member of the crew of the recently wrecked *Sibyl Marston*.

Helander told a reporter for the paper that he hoped "that his participation in the *R.D. Inman* disaster will be as beneficial for his future shipmates as was the first Jonah's historic submarine cruise."

The *Palestine*: A Rescuer's Reward

Inbound from Tacoma for the Golden Gate with 2,500 tons of British Columbian coal aboard, the clipper *Palestine*, captained by McCartney, struck the San Francisco Bar and was wrecked on June 26, 1891. She went down in eighty-five feet of water in just over an hour.

What work could be done went on over the next few weeks with some equipment, including a donkey engine, successfully salvaged from the submerged wreck. After everything that could be removed from the ship was salvaged, her hull was dynamited as a hazard to navigation.

She went down very close to where the *Elizabeth* sank just four months previous and the steamship *Escambia* was lost in 1882.

The drama of the wreck took an ironic turn when, a few days after the ill-fated *Palestine* was lost, her second mate, W.C. Walker, was arrested and jailed on a charge of petty larceny for stealing a pocket watch and chain from the engineer of the tug *Wizard*—one of the vessels that came to the *Palestine*'s aid when she was sinking.

The *May Flint*: A "Detested" and "Hideous" Party Crasher

A score of brightly lit ships were on hand in San Francisco Bay on the evening of September 8, 1900, in anticipation of the next day's celebration of the fiftieth anniversary of California's statehood.

The festivities took an unexpected turn when the four-masted bark *May Flint*, captained by Woodside, inbound from Seattle with five thousand tons of coal, entered the Golden Gate under full sail without a pilot. She became unmanageable in the light wind and, in full view of thousands of spectators, drifted onto the ram bow of the Spanish-American War veteran battleship USS *Iowa*.

A jagged gash ripped in her side, she drifted off the *Iowa*'s bow, caromed into the bark *Vidette* and turned turtle and sank in five minutes in the glare of half a dozen powerful searchlights.

"Among ships the *May Flint* was a leviathan," wrote the *San Francisco Call*. "Her history has been a strange one. Story after story of cruelty was recorded

Derided as "the ugliest square rigger that ever sailed the seas," the *May Flint* was lost in a spectacular collision in San Francisco Bay. *Courtesy of the San Francisco Maritime NHP.*

in her career. Those that had worked upon her told of the heartlessness of former commanders, and if she was one of the most imposing of the vessels which entered the bay, she also was one of the most thoroughly detested."

Launched in 1880 as the transatlantic passenger steamer *Persian Monarch*, the iron ship was later converted to sail. Years later, British maritime historian Basil Lubbock called her "hideous" and "the ugliest square rigger that ever sailed the seas."

Accused by the *May Flint*'s owners of "attempting a grandstand play," two years would pass before Captain Woodside received another command: the small lumber schooner *Alumna*.

THE *WALTER CLAXTON*: A FATAL FIRST VOYAGE

Bound for San Francisco with a cargo of 180,000 board feet of lumber, the bark *Walter Claxton* was struck by a heavy sea and capsized about ten miles off Mendocino on April 21, 1854.

Captain J.W. Folger, on his first voyage as master of the *Walter Claxton*, died with his ship. His body washed ashore five days after the wreck, about a half mile north of the Albion River, and was buried in Mendocino on the same day.

The fact that much of her lumber cargo was stowed on deck was seen as a possible cause of the wreck. Only three of the sixteen people aboard survived, and those only through the brave efforts of the crew of the schooner *Taranto*.

During the official investigation of the wreck, Captain Elisha Holmes of the schooner *Julius Pringle* testified that he had refused to go to the assistance of the *Walter Claxton* because "it would have taken three hours to place his vessel in a position to do so." The *Sacramento Daily Union* commented on Holmes's testimony, saying that "the *Taranto* got under way in one fourth the time and that not a soul would have been saved had not the latter vessel put out as she did."

The *Santa Rosa*: "Hugging the Shore"

At dawn on July 7, 1911, the Pacific Coast Steamship Company steamer *Santa Rosa* lay impaled on the rocks about one hundred yards off the beach six miles south of Point Arguello.

One of the best-known passenger steamers plying the California coast, the 2,416-ton ship was pounded by mountainous breakers through the day until dusk, when her master, Captain J.O. Faria, was persuaded by a delegation of passengers to load the boats and give them some chance of survival.

Twenty people paid with their lives when their lifeboats were swamped with the survivors rescued by a breeches buoy rigged by the crew of the nearby lifesaving station. Sixteen persons—eleven passengers and five sailors—were in the first boat that was launched, but it was quickly swamped, and all aboard were battered to death against the rocks or drowned. Another lifeboat with nineteen people aboard was launched and met the same fate. Fifteen of the people from that boat managed to reach shore alive, dazed and exhausted with some barely conscious.

Why did Captain Faria delay in launching the *Santa Rosa*'s lifeboats? That same question was put forward in the July 10 edition of the *San Francisco Call*, which carried an interview with one of the survivors of the wreck that appeared to provide an answer.

Twenty people died when a raging storm drove the steamer *Santa Rosa* ashore at Point Arguello on July 7, 1911. *Courtesy of the Golden Gate NRA.*

According to the *Santa Rosa*'s wireless operator, Barney Frankel, "We were in communication with the San Francisco office, via Point Arguello, from 7:30 a.m. until the ship broke in two. Our instructions were signed 'G.H. Higbee.' The last message ordered the captain to get out two more kedge anchors and hold her until the [tug] *President* came along. Captain Faria said, 'Kedge anchors lie damned. I'm going to get these passengers ashore before she goes to the bottom.'"

H.L. Higbee was the San Francisco–based general manager of the Pacific Coast Steamship Company. In Seattle at the time of the wreck, Higbee's name was apparently used to add weight to the directive by the assistant manager of the line on duty at time, J.H. Cooper.

Frankel's account was underscored in the same edition of the paper by survivor Mrs. Elitha Campbell, who had been traveling to Los Angeles aboard the *Santa Rosa* when she was lost. "We had been huddled together on the after deck for hours," she recounted. "When the lines parted and the ship swung around, everybody rushed forward. As I passed Captain Faria I heard him exclaim: 'I wish to God I had followed my own judgment instead of taking orders from the city. Every life would have been saved.' Captain Faria at once commenced to send passengers ashore."

Four weeks after the *Santa Rosa* was lost, Captain Faria and Third Mate E.J. Thomas were formally notified that they would have to stand trial on charges of "negligence and incompetence" for the loss of the ship. The official inquiry concluded, "Had he [Faria] got his lifeline on shore, and his boats and rafts out as soon as it was daylight, when, by all the testimony, the sea and swell were much less than in the afternoon, he could have landed his passengers on shore with much less risk to them, and he would have had a clear ship to work on, and, having no passengers to take care of, he could have given all his attention to getting afloat, if possible."

After a two-month investigation, both Faria and Thomas lost their licenses for a year.

The *San Francisco Call* responded to the finding with the charge that the two officers had been turned into scapegoats as the Pacific Coast Steamship Company had escaped any criticism for its "practice of hugging the shore in making coastwise voyages." The paper also asked why "no comment was made upon the flood of wireless telegrams haggling over the price of rescue that were hurled at Captain Faria from the office in this city after the vessel struck." All of the blame, the *Call* charged, "is placed upon the shoulders of the two officers."

The wreck of the *Santa Rosa* ended the career of a fine ship that, over the preceding twenty years, had completed 1,110 trips up and down the coast without mishap.

A few days later, the tragedy claimed its last victim when it was reported that a young woman in Berkeley, sixteen-year-old Edith May Carlisle, collapsed and died after hearing that her older brother, William, was aboard the *Santa Rosa*. In a tragic twist of irony, he had survived the wreck by clinging to a piece of floating wreckage until he was able to make it to shore, exhausted but alive.

The *San Benito*: A "Hopeless Wreck"

Of her crew of forty-three, seven drowned when a series of navigational errors put the steam collier *San Benito* ashore in a strong gale just north of Point Reyes at 1:15 a.m. on November 22, 1896.

The death toll would have been much higher had not a four-man boat crew from the steam schooner *Point Arena* risked their lives in making several trips to the wreck to rescue four officers and crewmen clinging to the doomed ship's rigging.

"As hopeless a wreck as was ever seen on the Pacific Coast," wrote the *San Francisco Call*, the ship split in half and was gradually ground to pieces on the rocks with little left to salvage when the storm abated.

The four Point Arena crewmen—First Mate L.E. Olsen and seamen Peter Anderson, Andrew Lillel and Axel Hendricksen—were later recommended to Congress for their heroism and received Gold Lifesaving Medals.

As for the *San Benito*'s captain, William Smith, and first mate, R. Zolling, both had their licenses revoked for "gross negligence and unskillful management of the collier" in a decision handed down after a lengthy investigation conducted by the U.S. Board of Investigators of Steam Vessels.

The *San Benito* was owned by the Southern Pacific Railroad and was headed for San Francisco with five thousand tons of coal loaded at Tacoma when she was lost.

THE *KING PHILIP*: A CREW DEFENDS ITS CAPTAIN

The *King Philip*, a 1,194-ton, three-masted, Maine-built medium clipper, was wrecked on January 25, 1878, on Ocean Beach.

Her twenty-two-year career ended when she was driven ashore on the tide in a light wind after the steam tug that had towed her out of San Francisco Bay had to drop its towline to go to the aid of another ship, whose captain had been suddenly killed in a deck accident.

The wreck was left in place, and the following day, the ship was sold at auction for $1,050 to an enterprising San Francisco businessman named John Molloy, who salvaged the metal fastenings, cut down the masts and sails and had the hulk blown up with a black powder charge.

Sometime in the late 1890s, a crowd of Sunday excursionists enjoys a Sunday afternoon at Ocean Beach, located just to the south of the entrance to San Francisco Bay. In the background, the seven-story Cliff House restaurant perches on the bluff overlooking the treacherous Seal Rocks. *Courtesy of the Golden Gate NRA.*

A few days after the ship was lost, a rumor that the ship's master, Captain Keller, was drunk at the time of the wreck was dismissed as "false and malicious" by thirty-six crewmen of the *King Philip* who put their names to a letter printed in the *Daily Alta California* defending their captain. "At no time during our connection with him," they wrote, "have we seen him in the state mentioned, or unable to perform his duty as a master or a thorough seaman, which he undoubtedly is."

What remained was eventually covered by the sand, but the ship's timbers have been uncovered at low tide numerous times over the past 135 years.

The *Brooklyn*: A Broken Back and a Single Survivor

Heavy seas were running and heavy rain falling when the 334-ton, double-ended steam schooner *Brooklyn* stood out of Humboldt Bay for San Francisco with a deck load of lumber on the morning of November 8, 1930.

The *Brooklyn*, built in Aberdeen, Washington, in 1901, struck the Humboldt Bar so sharply that her back was immediately broken and she started to go to pieces.

Coast Guardsmen from the local lifesaving station were hampered in their rescue efforts by the debris and deck cargo that surrounded the wreck. Sadly, her first mate proved to be the only survivor. He was found several days later floating on a hatch cover several miles from where the tired, old *Brooklyn* was wrecked.

The *Alcatraz*: A Deadly Habit

The lumber-laden steam schooner *Alcatraz* was wrecked on May 2, 1917, on the beach near Greenwood, ten miles north of Point Arena on the coast of Mendocino County. According to contemporary reports, the sea was "as smooth as glass on a moonlit night" when the wreck occurred.

The cause of the wreck was the subject of much speculation, some of it involving alcohol, while others said that Captain Krause's fondness for

The steam schooner *Alcatraz*, smashed to pieces in the surf at Greenwood. *Courtesy of the Pacific Grove Museum of Natural History.*

habitually hugging the shoreline on his way south to San Francisco was the reason the ship was lost.

Owned by the E.L. White Lumber Company, the *Alcatraz* had sailed in the coastal lumber trade for thirty years before she was lost.

THE *FRANCOIS COPPEE*: A MAIDEN VOYAGE ENDS IN TRAGEDY

The steel, three-masted bark *Francois Coppee* piled onto an underwater pinnacle at Bird Rock, about five hundred yards off the northern end of the Point Reyes peninsula, on November 20, 1903.

Her master had managed to sail the French-flagged ship all the way from New South Wales, Australia, where she'd taken aboard a cargo of coal for San Francisco, but his navigational skills proved faulty when he mistook the head of Tomales for that of Point Lobos, driving the *Francois Coppee* onto the underwater rocks.

Nine of the doomed ship's crew panicked and deserted, quickly lowering the ship's only boat and sailing off, leaving their fellows virtually helpless. The remaining fifteen members of the crew, including the captain, went over the side and tried to swim through the towering breakers to shore. Only four of the men made it, spending the next two days on the beach until they were discovered by a rancher looking for a lost cow. Locals responded quickly, and the survivors were carried by wagon to a farmhouse four miles away, where they were cared for until they could be transported to San Francisco.

Two weeks later, the *Los Angeles Herald* reported, "The French bark *Francois Coppee* is breaking up rapidly. All that was left yesterday of the ship was the bow. Later the steel plates parted and the wreck gave evidence of falling apart. Casks of wine, clothing and debris are floating ashore."

The bodies of the eleven men who died trying to make it to shore were later recovered and buried on the beach. The fate of the nine deserters remains unknown.

THE *HANALEI*: A HERO AND HIS FLASHLIGHT

Originally built for the Hawaiian sugar trade, the steam schooner *Hanalei* worked the route hauling lumber between various Northern California ports and San Francisco Bay, with an occasional trip to San Pedro.

Sailing from Eureka, California, with sixty persons on board and a cargo of cut lumber, live cattle, sheep and hogs, *Hanalei* was lost on November

23, 1914, running aground on Duxbury Reef opposite the Marconi Wireless Station at Bolinas.

Fifty years after the wreck of the steam schooner *Hanalei*, her former radio operator, Loren Lovejoy, reviews newspaper accounts of the 1913 disaster. *Author's collection.*

The battering of wreckage, the loose lumber cargo and the choking effect of the ship's diesel fuel on the water took a deadly toll, as twenty-three passengers and crew members drowned while struggling to reach the shore. A number were saved when the crew of the U.S. Revenue Cutter *McCulloch* pulled them from the water, with a handful of others washed alive onto the beach after hours in the water, struggling in the swells and the floating wreckage.

The *Hanalei*'s wireless operator, twenty-two-year-old Loren Lovejoy, stayed aboard the stricken ship and used a flashlight to maintain Morse code communication with the Marconi station after the ship's radio aerial and equipment were put out of commission by the hammering sea.

Lovejoy was later recognized for his heroism, as were Captain J.S. Clark and Captain J.L. Nutter of the Point Bonita and Fort Point Life-Saving Stations, respectively.

THE *COLUMBIA* AND THE *ALICE BUCK*: A YOUNG GIRL AND AN UNKNOWN SAILOR

The July 21, 1907 loss of the San Francisco and Portland Steamship Company coastal steamer *Columbia* remains one of the Pacific Coast's worst—and most poignant—maritime disasters.

Headed north from San Francisco bound for Puget Sound, the *Columbia*, captained by Peter A. Doran, steamed at top speed through the fog and went to the bottom off Eureka in just eleven minutes after being rammed by the lumber-laden steam schooner *San Pedro*.

According to one survivor's account, "The crew was at the boats, cutting and slashing at the lashings, and doing their utmost to launch them while the frenzied passengers ran everywhere begging to be saved. Some kneeled on the deck and said their last prayers, men clasped their wives in their arms, and mothers gathered their children about them. We waited for the end, which, by intuition, we all knew was at hand."

Captain Doran recalled that as the *Columbia* sank, he urged the passengers to remain calm with his final words: "Goodbye and God bless you."

Aboard the *Columbia* on her way to visit her brother in Portland was sixteen-year-old Maybelle Watson of Berkeley, who was later lauded for her heroism during the wreck.

Thrown into the water when her lifeboat was swamped in the sinking ship's vortex, Watson saved the life of Emma Griese, a young schoolteacher from Cleveland, Ohio, who was struggling in the water, having put on her lifejacket back to front.

Watson, though completely exhausted, fought for the better part of an hour to keep the dazed woman's head out of the water until they were both picked up by another of the *Columbia*'s lifeboats.

The *Columbia* carried 251 passengers and crew, 88 of whom died when she was wrecked. Among those lost were honeymooners George Liggett, twenty-five, and his twenty-two-year-old wife of seven days, as well as schoolteacher Miss Margaret McKeaney (University of California, class of 1904), who was on her way to a ten-day vacation in Portland.

The loss of the American ship *Alice Buck* provided another example of gallantry and sacrifice when she ran aground in the pounding surf at the foot of a bluff near Spanishtown at Half Moon Bay on September 26, 1881.

Outbound from New York, she had rounded Cape Horn with a cargo of railroad iron consigned to the Northern Pacific Railroad in Portland. Once unloaded there, she was to have taken on a full cargo of grain under charter for Europe.

A total of eleven men died in the wreck of the *Alice Buck*, a death toll that undoubtedly would have been higher had it not been for the heroism of several of her crew who braved the surf in attempts, both futile and successful, to save their fellows.

The *Sacramento Daily Union* chronicled the sacrifice of one sailor, who, to this day, has never been identified.

The unknown seaman "managed to reach the narrow strip of beach at the foot of the cliff and, after recovering his breath, struck out into the waves again and brought safely to land another shipmate. He again bravely struck out and succeeded in rescuing another sinking sailor, but a third attempt proved fatal to the gallant fellow, for he sank beneath the water, and was seen no more."

CHAPTER 3

FOG, ROCKS AND SHOALS

In June 1579, Sir Francis Drake, deftly exploring the west coast of North America in the name of Queen Elizabeth I of England, penned a graphic indictment of California's ragged coastline. He wrote that it was, quite simply, a place beset by "thicke mists"; "vile, thicke and stinking fogges"; and "contrary windes."

More than 250 years later, Richard Henry Dana underscored Drake's assessment in his classic work *Two Years Before the Mast*. The Harvard-educated Dana, who never attempted to conceal his dislike for California, wrote of the fickleness of the coast's weather with its wind—the fabled southeaster—"the bane of the California coast," its "heavy seas and fogs" and jagged rocks "as large as those of Nahant or Newport."

One of the many ships lost on those rocks in one of those "vile, thicke and stinking fogges" was the British-flag iron bark *Coya*. Lashed by a heavy sea, she went aground in the fog near Pigeon Point on November 24, 1866, at a cost of twenty-seven of the thirty passengers and crew aboard, including Captain Jeffries's wife and child.

The doomed bark was laden with coal from Sydney, New South Wales, for San Francisco and was later determined to be sixty miles off course when she was wrecked.

The three numbed survivors—Walter Cooper, G. Byrnes and Barstow, the first mate—made it to shore, where they huddled together on the sand until morning. At dawn, they were able to walk to the nearby White House ranch, where they were fed and sheltered.

The next day, the trio returned to the beach to search for other survivors but found only the body of the captain's wife, Mrs. Jeffries, which they buried "as well as the state of things would permit," according to their account.

The *Coya* herself was gone, but among the debris washed ashore was a medical instrument chest, a number of carpenter's tools and, poignantly, "the green shawl in which Mrs. Jeffries had undoubtedly wrapped her little boy."

THE *MARY D. POMEROY*: A "SPLENDID VESSEL"

Exactly one week before Christmas 1879 and almost two hundred years after Drake's assessment of the dangerously configured coastline, every one of the fifteen people aboard the schooner *Mary D. Pomeroy* was lost when the ship was wrecked off Point Reyes.

The 114-ton schooner, launched almost six months to the day before she was lost, was employed on the route between Crescent City and San Francisco.

Remembered as a "splendid-looking vessel," the schooner was built in Mendocino at Thomas Peterson's Little River shipyard and had placed second in that year's July 4 Mariners Regatta held on San Francisco Bay.

No bodies were ever recovered from the wreck, and efforts by the steamer *Monterey* to tow the capsized hulk to port came to naught.

As for the cause of the wreck, no one will ever know.

THE *VISCATA*: A LEGAL INJUSTICE

On March 7, 1868, the 204-foot-long *Viscata*, outbound for London with about six hundred tons of wheat, went ashore and was wrecked at Point Lobos, near the entrance to San Francisco Bay.

For weeks after the wreck, accusations flew back and forth in the local press about whom or what was responsible for the loss of the four-year-old, 1,065-ton, Liverpool-built ship. The primary target was Captain William

The hull and cargo of the British-flag *Viscata* were sold at auction after repeated attempts to salvage the ship failed. The ship was wrecked near the mouth of San Francisco Bay on March 7, 1868. *Courtesy of the San Francisco Maritime NHP.*

Jollife, the San Francisco Bar pilot, who was vigorously defended by the *Viscata*'s master and officers and who testified at the investigation following the wreck that "the loss of the ship was entirely due to the breaking of the stock of the anchor."

The *Daily Alta California* noted, "Before the fact of the disabling of the anchor could be ascertained, the ship, which was drifting all the time, with a momentary expectation that she would bring up with the anchor holding, was out of any possibility of being saved." The paper continued: "We call attention to this case, as it has excited considerable feeling, and it is possible that injustice may be done through an anxiety to make an example of somebody."

Despite a heated defense of Captain Jollife, the Board of Pilot Commissioners voted to deprive him of his pilot's license. The board's decision was challenged when it was cited before a local judge "to show cause why they should not reverse their action in the matter of depriving pilot Jollife of his license for the loss of the *Viscata*."

Most of the *Viscata*'s cargo of wheat was salvaged, and a week later, her hull was sold at auction to Stevens, Baker & Co. for $22,500.

THE *EASTPORT*: "DEPRIVED OF A MOTHER'S CARE"

Mr. John Armstrong lost his wife and two of his three children when the steamer *Eastport* ran onto a reef just north of the Point Arena Lighthouse in the early morning hours of July 23, 1875. The ship was bound from Coos Bay to San Francisco.

Mrs. Armstrong and the two children were aboard one of the ship's lifeboats that capsized immediately after being launched. They were the only passengers lost in the disaster.

"All the passengers rushed for the boats hanging over the side of the steamer. Unfortunately, one end of it broke loose, precipitating them into the water, but all succeeded in saving themselves by clinging to the boat, with the exception of the lady and two children above mentioned," reported the *Los Angeles Herald*.

The battered remains of the ship, which had originally been insured for $60,000, were bought at auction by Mr. John Rosenfield of San Francisco for $300; her cargo of four hundred tons of coal went for all of $10.

In December, Armstrong filed a suit against the *Eastport*'s owners, claiming that the wrecking of the ship and deaths of his wife and two children "occurred through the carelessness of the defendants." Asking for $15,000 in damages, he claimed that he had been "deprived of the affection of his wife and two children" and that his surviving four-year-old son had been "deprived of a mother's care."

No record of the suit has been found indicating whether Armstrong or his son received their judgment.

THE *SAMUEL S. LEWIS*: A SURVIVOR SAVED FOR BIGGER THINGS

It was Duxbury Reef, north of the Golden Gate near the town of Bolinas, that claimed the steamship *Samuel S. Lewis*, captained by Sparrow, on April 9, 1853. Built in Philadelphia just two years before, the ship—also known as the *S.S. Lewis*—flew the house flag of the Independent Line.

Aboard the ship (which was carrying 385 passengers) was future Civil War commander William T. Sherman, who had only a few months earlier resigned his commission as a captain in the U.S. Army and was bound for

The steamer *Samuel S. Lewis*. This lithograph was published shortly before she was wrecked on April 9, 1853. *Courtesy of the Golden Gate NHP.*

San Francisco to assume the position of branch manager of the Lucas, Turner & Co. Bank.

The wreck occurred about six miles north of where the steamer *Tennessee* went aground just a month earlier. There was no loss of life in the wreck, but the ship was a total loss.

THE *WESTERN SHORE*:
LOST IN "NOT UNFAVORABLE" WEATHER

Bound from Seattle to San Francisco and laden with 2,040 tons of coal, the 183-foot, full-rigged ship *Western Shore*, like the *Samuel S. Lewis* before her, plowed bow-on into Duxbury Reef on the evening of July 9, 1878.

She sank within three hours, with only the masts with all sails still set protruding from the water. The circumstances of her loss were never fully explained, as reported in the *Sacramento Daily Union* of July 11. The wreck, the paper wrote, "is difficult to account for, as at the time the ship struck both the Farallon and Point Reyes lights were plainly visible, and although there was a stiff breeze blowing, the weather was not unfavorable. The ship was under full sail, and going at the rate of twelve knots when she struck the reef…The ship is fast going to pieces and will soon be a total wreck."

The *Western Shore* was valued at $80,000 and was considered a fast sailer, having previously made two "first class" passages to Europe.

THE *LA FELIZ*: SARDINES ON THE ROCKS

There were no casualties when the *La Feliz* was caught in a heavy sea and smashed against an outcropping of rock near Watsonville, about two miles north of the Santa Cruz Light on October 1, 1924.

Heavy seas smash the steam schooner *La Feliz* ashore near the Santa Cruz Light with a hold full of canned sardines, October 1, 1924. *Courtesy of the Pacific Grove Museum of Natural History.*

The 102-ton steam schooner, built in 1904, was headed for San Francisco with a cargo of canned sardines—insured by the Firemen's Fund—that had been loaded at Monterey. The *La Feliz* was found to be running too close to shore when the wreck occurred.

Attempts to salvage the cargo were temporarily thwarted by an artichoke rancher who held off salvors hired by the insurance company with a Winchester rifle in an attempt to extort $500 from them before he would allow them to cross his land and reach the wreck.

The *Frank Jones*: "Too Close to the Rocks"

The ship *Frank Jones* was under tow of the tug *Monarch*, outbound on the afternoon of March 30, 1877, from San Francisco in ballast for Manila to load cargo there for New York and Boston.

A strong northwest gale was blowing when the hawser snapped. Another was quickly rigged, but it and a third also parted under the strain. Both anchors were dropped, but their cable proved to be too short to secure the 1,453-ton ship.

The *Monarch* was finally able to secure a line aboard the *Frank Jones*, but her best efforts weren't enough to prevent the ship's fatal drift onto the rocks. Her pilot tried to avert catastrophe by getting sail on her, but she was carried ashore about two hundred yards south of Fort Point.

"There is scarcely any hope of saving her," wrote the *Daily Alta California*. "The tug kept too near the south shore…and the ship was too close to the rocks. She had no cargo and was in no condition to maneuver on a lee shore."

Attempts to bring her off the beach stretched over several months but were unsuccessful despite favorable conditions. She was eventually stripped of her spars, fittings and rigging and sold at the Merchant's Exchange for $4,750.

A few weeks before she was wrecked, the *Frank Jones* had completed her third voyage to San Francisco from New York, a 126-day passage with general merchandise consigned to several Bay Area businesses.

THE *SAN RAFAEL*: LOST IN THE FOG

Under the command of Captain John Mackenzie, the *San Rafael* sank near Alcatraz Island on November 30, 1901, after colliding in the fog with the steam ferry *Sausalito*.

Both vessels were owned by the same company, the North Pacific Coast Railway. The steamer was bound from San Francisco across the Bay with passengers for Sausalito. Both vessels were proceeding slowly and ringing fog bells.

Both captains reportedly realized the other ship was near and had ordered the engines reversed, but it was too late to prevent a collision.

Quick work by a fireman on the *San Rafael* prevented a potentially catastrophic explosion when he reentered the fire room and braved neck-deep water to open the bleed valve on the ship's boilers.

Approximately twenty minutes after the collision, the *San Rafael* sank in about 120 feet of water. Captain Mackenzie was the last person to leave the ship before she went to the bottom.

Several weeks after the sinking, an extensive investigation by a board of inquiry found that both captains were at fault, and the licenses of both were suspended, though Mackenzie's ticket was reinstated the following January.

THE *J.B. STETSON*: A FATAL ESTIMATE

Working her way through one of the thickest fogs ever recorded at Monterey, the steam schooner *J.B. Stetson* went onto a rocky reef off Monterey in the early morning hours of September 3, 1934.

Her bow smashed in, the ship began to take on water immediately, with her engine room flooding and her crew scrambling on deck in their pajamas. Her master, Captain F.W. Hubner, had estimated he was at Cypress Point, three miles south of the entrance to Monterey Bay. He turned the ship onto the shore near the golf course on 17-Mile Drive. Repeated soundings of the ship's horn roused the course's matron, Mrs. C.F. Cuthrie, who telephoned the U.S. Coast Guard Station at Monterey.

The USCGC *Daphne* was immediately dispatched and took aboard the steam schooner's crew and the ship's mongrel mascot, Flossie. Neither the ship nor her $5,000 cargo of general merchandise could be salvaged, with splintered debris from the wreck washing ashore for weeks afterward.

Outbound from Long Beach for Monterey when she was wrecked, the *J.B. Stetson* went aground only one hundred yards from where the steamer *Flavel* was lost eleven years earlier.

The 835-ton ship was named for the scion of the iconic J.B. Stetson Hat Company.

THE *ESCAMBIA*: A "LACK OF JUDGMENT"

The 291-foot steamer *Escambia* capsized and sank, taking twenty people down with her, at 7:00 p.m. on June 19, 1881.

The British-flag ship, heavily laden with a cargo of wheat for the Cape Verde Islands, was on the south edge of the San Francisco Bar when she was struck by a heavy swell that rolled her over.

The *Escambia* was riding high, as her ballast tanks had been emptied so she could take on more cargo, while her deck was reportedly piled with coal as high as her bridge deck.

The British Board of Trade's inquiry found that Captain Purvis, one of only four survivors of the wreck, "was to blame for taking the vessel to sea under that condition, having acted simply through lack of judgment."

The only reason his license wasn't permanently revoked was the fact that he had "made every effort to save life after the vessel capsized."

THE *BREMEN*: NOW YOU HEAR IT, NOW YOU DON'T

Her hold filled with cases of malt whiskey, the three-masted, English-flag square-rigger *Bremen* was 118 days out from Liverpool when she encountered heavy fog while approaching the mouth of the San Francisco Bay on October 16, 1882.

The ship went head-on to the northwest side of South Farallon Island, the after part going under water and the vessel "striking heavily" in a severe swell.

The three-master *Bremen* "struck heavily" and was lost at the mouth of San Francisco Bay on October 16, 1882. *Courtesy of the San Francisco Maritime NHP.*

"It appears to be established by the testimony of the officers and crew of the wrecked ship *Bremen* that the fog-horn was not heard by them until after she had struck on the Farallons," wrote the *Sacramento Daily Union.*

A San Francisco newspaper suggested that "as a possible explanation of this, that sometimes sound is acted upon by fog in the most eccentric and mysterious ways, and that the people of the *Bremen* may not have heard the horn, even though it was being blown persistently. It is no doubt true that sound is sometimes acted upon by fog in this way."

The ship had originally been built in 1858 as a steamer by Caird & Co. of Greenock, Scotland. Fortunately, no lives were lost in the wreck.

THE *NEW YORK*: A "HOODOO" BY ANY NAME

The loss of the USS *Maine* in Havana Harbor and the ramp-up to the start of the Spanish-American War all but pushed news of the March

13, 1898 wreck of the ship *New York* onto the back pages of newspapers across the state.

The three-masted ship was lost when her master couldn't get his bearings and the ship ran aground in a thick fog about three hundred yards offshore at Half Moon Bay, about twenty-five miles up the coast from San Francisco.

Laden with a $500,000 cargo of raw silk and general merchandise loaded in Hong Kong, the ship was built as the *T.F. Oakes* and, according to the Los *Angeles Herald*, "had a reputation while under that name of being a hoodoo ship that was always in trouble of some kind."

On one occasion, the paper reported, "Nearly all the crew was stricken with scurvy, and after a voyage of 200 days from China, she was steered into New York harbor by Mrs. Reed, the wife of her captain."

THE *BOBOLINK*: "FOR SALE AT A SACRIFICE"

On March 24, 1898, the two-masted schooner *Bobolink* ended her thirty-year career hard and fast on Kent's Point at the south end of Mendocino Bay.

The schooner, built in 1868, was outbound for San Francisco with a deckload of cut lumber for the Mendocino Lumber Company.

Seaman Peter Nelson, a native of Sweden, was lost when the lumber schooner *Bobolink* went onto the rocks at Kent's Point south of Mendocino Bay. *Courtesy of the Kelley House Museum.*

Just as she reached the mouth of the harbor, the wind died, and her master, Captain Nelson, ordered her anchor dropped close in shore. A short time later, she was struck by a sudden violent squall. Her anchor dragged, and she went onto the rocks with her bottom nearly torn out.

"Everything possible was done to save her," wrote the *San Francisco Call*. "An attempt was made to get her off, and while the men were at work, one of the boats capsized, and Peter Nelson was drowned…and while the vessel will probably be a total loss, the chances are that the cargo will be saved."

The force with which she went ashore, the paper said, "nearly tore the entire bottom out of her, but to look at her as she now lies in smooth water no one would ever think but she was lying at anchor ready to discharge her cargo. The cargo will be saved, but the wreck of the vessel is now 'For Sale at a Sacrifice.'"

THE *CRESCENT CITY*: AN UNCALIBRATED COMPASS AND "DEFECTIVE EYESIGHT"

Fortunately, no lives were lost when the *Crescent City*, battered by a severe southwest gale, grounded on Fish Rock off the coast of Mendocino on January 30, 1903.

The ship was valued at $45,000, but the shattered wreck was sold a week later at a Merchant's Exchange auction for only $700.

Fast aground on Fish Rock, the steam schooner *Crescent City* was a total loss, pounded to pieces in the surf. *Courtesy of the Pacific Grove Museum of Natural History.*

The *San Francisco Call* later reported that the official government investigation determined that while the crew was to be commended for their heroism during the disaster, the wreck was caused, at least in part, by written evidence that the ship's owners had repeatedly ignored repeated requests by her captain that the ship's compass be recalibrated.

In addition, the investigation concluded, the outcome of the incident wasn't helped by the "peculiarly defective eyesight" of Otto Olsen, the *Crescent City*'s first mate, who was on the bridge when the ship went aground.

The *Newsboy*: Wrecked on the Humboldt Bar

The steam schooner *Newsboy* was built in 1888 and was sold to Captain Robert Dollar, the future shipping magnate, in 1892.

Sold again, she was wrecked while crossing the Humboldt River Bar on March 31, 1906. An Associated Press story in the *Los Angeles Herald* detailed her loss: "Outward bound for San Francisco with a cargo of lumber, the steamer *Newsboy* was struck by a heavy sea while in the south channel, with the result that she lost her rudder and deckload."

Completely helpless, "the *Newsboy* blew signals of distress and the tug *Ranger* answered the call. After some maneuvering she got a line aboard the *Newsboy* and started to bring her through the bay's entrance when she met the steamer *Wasp* from Eureka to Portland."

According to the newspaper report, the tug blew one whistle for the *Wasp* to get out of the way, but the steamer paid no attention to the warning. The collision stove in the tug's starboard bow and toppled her smokestack.

The *Ranger*, the paper said, "was then forced to abandon the *Newsboy* and immediately got out of the way to prevent the hawser fouling with her propeller. She clocked about 7 o'clock. The *Wasp* failed in an attempt to get a line aboard the *Newsboy*, and the latter finally anchored at the end of the south jetty, while the *Wasp*, after coming in to the bay, put to sea."

The *Newsboy*'s crew abandoned ship that evening "breaking the shred of hope that there is any chance to save her."

SHIPWRECKS OF THE CALIFORNIA COAST

THE *DORA BLUHM*: LOST FOR WANT OF A LIGHT

On May 25, 1910, the combination of heavy weather and navigational error put the schooner *Dora Bluhm* on the rocks on Santa Rosa Island, where she broke her back.

The three-master was seven days out of Coos Bay for San Pedro with a cargo of 350,000 board feet of lumber consigned to the Golden State Lumber Company.

For several years, she had been engaged in cod fishing before being employed in the lumber trade.

The schooner went ashore near the wreck of the British steamer *Golden Horn*, which was lost in 1892 with 4,500 tons of coal, and the remains of the *Crown of England*, another collier, wrecked in 1896. The *Los Angeles Herald* opined, "All three wrecks might have been avoided by a light on Anacapa Island, which has been recommended by the Lighthouse Board."

The schooner was owned by the Pacific States Trading Company of San Francisco and was built at Port Blakeley, Washington, in 1883.

THE *HARVARD*:
PRIDE OF THE COASTAL PASSENGER FLEET

The *Harvard*—and her twin sister, the *Yale*—were popular coastal passenger steamers that plied the route between Los Angeles and San Francisco on a four-trips-a-week schedule for the Los Angeles Steamship Co., a subsidiary of the Matson Navigation Co.

The turbine-powered ship served in World War I as the USS *Charles* ferrying troops between Southampton and Le Havre and served along the Atlantic seaboard before being reassigned to the West Coast.

For her war service, the *Harvard* was awarded corporal's stripes, which were affixed to her forward funnel and remained there to the end, which turned out to be May 30, 1931.

She was on her 972nd trip at three thirty that clear morning when she went aground at twenty knots, settling on an even keel on the rocks only one hundred yards off Point Arguello, about sixty miles north of Santa Barbara.

Captain Lewis Hilsinger, who was filling in for the *Harvard's* regular master, ordered a distress call sounded and an SOS sent out immediately. Several ships responded, including the freighter *San Anselmo*, which altered course to come to her aid, unloaded her five hundred passengers and, later, safely transferred them to the cruiser USS *Louisville*.

The entrepreneurial rancher who owned the property immediately fronting the wreck saw an opportunity to make a fast buck and reportedly made quite a killing by charging fifty cents a carload to curiosity seekers wanting to view the stranded ship. According to one account, between twenty thousand and thirty thousand cars took him up on his offer.

Theories abounded about why the *Harvard* was wrecked, with a negligent lookout, faulty steering gear and an exceptionally strong inshore current topping the list. Some theorists even alleged that the ship's log had been altered to cover the fact that she was too close to shore.

Whatever the case, the *Harvard*, once the pride of California's coastal passenger fleet, soon broke up and was no more.

In an ironic footnote, the *Harvard's* initial distress call was sounded on a steam whistle that had been salvaged from the *Santa Rosa* and installed on the *Harvard's* aft stack. The *Santa Rosa*, another popular coastal passenger steamer, had been wrecked twenty years earlier, ironically also at Point Arguello.

The *Yosemite*: A Floating Bomb

Owned by Pope & Talbot and one of the first steam schooners equipped with radio, the 927-ton *Yosemite* spent her ten-year career with "P&T" ferrying cut lumber, cargo and passengers between the company's Pacific Northwest mills and San Francisco.

She was laden with a cargo of twenty-five tons of dynamite and blasting caps when she went onto the rocks in a heavy fog at Point Reyes in the early morning hours of February 7, 1926.

Captain Silvia was able to back off, but severe damage below the waterline caused her to fill quickly and begin to heel over on her starboard side.

As the crew-laden boats were lowered, a distress signal was sent out that drew the steam schooner *Willamette*, which altered course and steamed toward the stricken *Yosemite*. She rescued the steam schooner's crew members and carried them on to San Francisco.

Pope & Talbot had chartered the tug *Sea Ranger* to make for the wreck and assist in any salvage operation, but an attempt to tow the *Yosemite* to San Francisco failed when the hawser snapped and the ship broke free and went ashore on Ocean Beach, near the Cliff House, at the foot of Fulton Street.

Like virtually all wrecks at the Cliff House, thousands of spectators gathered over the next few days to view the shattered *Yosemite*, collect souvenirs from the debris scattered along the beach and pose for photographs.

THE *COMMODORE RODGERS* AND THE *ATLANTIC*: WHALERS ASHORE

Far from her homeport of New Bedford, Massachusetts, on a Pacific whaling expedition, the *Commodore Rodgers* was riding increasingly rising swells off Monterey Bay when a sudden southwest squall caused the ship to lose her mizzenmast and go ashore on the morning of November 19, 1836.

Within a week, the ship had been pounded to pieces. Her masts, rigging and fittings sold for $15,000 at a public auction, while her cargo of nine hundred barrels of valuable whale oil went for $10 each.

Curious locals examine the wreckage of the whaler *Atlantic*, scattered along the shore near the Cliff House. *Author's collection.*

The loss of the whaler provided another boost of sorts to the local economy when one of the survivors of the wreck, seaman William McGlone, decided to give up the sea and, later, establish California's first brewery.

Fifty years later, not a spar remained standing after the whaling bark *Atlantic* was caught in a heavy swell and went aground about two hundred yards off Ocean Beach, about a mile and a half below the Cliff House. Twenty-seven men died in the December 17, 1886 wreck, while another eleven, including Captain Thomas Warren and the first mate, survived. None of the bodies of those who were lost was ever recovered.

The *Atlantic* was built in 1851, and the poor condition of her hull led to the ship breaking apart quickly in the pounding waves. Her wreckage was scattered for three miles along the beach.

THE *PARALLEL*: A SHATTERING BLAST

Outbound from San Francisco Bay to Astoria, Oregon, on January 12, 1887, the schooner *Parallel* made little headway in heavy weather and contrary tides, making it only as far as Land's End before going ashore near the Seal Rocks below the Cliff House.

The crew abandoned the vessel and watched from the shore as the cargo of forty tons of blasting powder, kerosene, pig iron and hay exploded at about 1:30 a.m. in a blast that was felt as far away as Sacramento.

Though the exact cause of the explosion was never determined, many concluded it was probably ignited by the oil lamps left burning aboard before the schooner was wrecked.

Amazingly, no lives were lost and only a few minor injuries were recorded, but the explosion demolished the entire north wing of the Cliff House tavern.

The following day, an estimated eighty thousand curious San Franciscans visited the site to view the damage and what little was left of the schooner.

A VICTORY VANISHES AND FOUR LIBERTIES LOST

When her cargo of explosives blew up, disintegrating the Liberty ship *E.A. Bryan* at Port Chicago, California, on July 17, 1944, the blast shattered the nearby Victory-class freighter *Quinault Victory* in a cataclysm that created a shock wave that broke windows more than two hundred miles away.

The Victory ship was literally blown out of the water, torn into sections and thrown in several directions, with the ship's mangled stern landing upside down in the water more than five hundred feet away. The blast destroyed most of the buildings at the naval magazine; killed 320 sailors, Coast Guardsmen and civilians; and injured another 390 people.

The *E.A. Bryan*'s cargo consisted of more than five thousand tons of antiaircraft ammunition, aerial high explosives, fragmentation cluster bombs and depth charges destined for the South Pacific.

The 7,176-ton Liberty-type ship *Henry Bergh*, under the command of Captain Joseph Chambers, was bound from the South Pacific to San Francisco via Honolulu with a crew of 100 and more than 1,400 U.S. Navy personnel being rotated home.

In the early morning hours of May 31, 1944, after more than thirty-six hours of navigating through an exceptionally heavy fog without an opportunity to take a navigational fix, the ship went onto the rocks of South Farallon Island.

The discipline of the crew and passengers was evident; only two men were injured and thirty-five treated for exposure, as those aboard were shuttled ashore twenty-five at a time in each of the vessel's eight lifeboats. By the time the first rescue craft had arrived on the scene at 8:00 a.m., six hundred men had been landed.

By early afternoon, all hands had been safely picked up. A volunteer crew remained on board as a tug attempted, without success, to haul off the *Henry Bergh*. The effort proved fruitless, as her back was broken and the hull split in half just aft of the superstructure. No salvage was attempted.

The ship was owned by the War Shipping Administration, operated by the Norton Lilly Company and chartered to the U.S. Navy for use as a transport.

On July 11, 1949, an impenetrable fog and poor navigation combined to force the Greek-registered, Liberty-type freighter *Ioannis G. Kulukundis* aground at Point Arguello, two miles south of Surf.

Salvors tried for four days to refloat the tramp ship, but she worked deeper and deeper into the sand, eventually breaking in two when she split just forward of the bridge.

The 7,176-ton tramper was carrying a full cargo of wheat from Vancouver, British Columbia, for Capetown. The cargo proved to be problematic when it started to expand and made the job of salvaging it extremely difficult.

The *Dominator*, another Greek-flag Liberty, was southbound from Vancouver, British Columbia, via Portland, Oregon, with a cargo of ten thousand tons of wheat and beef for Algiers on March 13, 1961, when she went aground at the foot of the cliffs at Palos Verdes, about twelve miles north of San Pedro.

The ship was scheduled to take on bunker fuel at the Port of Long Beach and was not equipped with radar when she was lost. The *Dominator* was abandoned after several attempts at salvage failed and, months later, the hull broke in half.

The ship was launched as the *Melville Jacoby* in March 1944 at the Walsh-Kaiser shipyard in Providence, Rhode Island, but all that's left of her rests today at the foot of the cliffs at Palos Verdes.

What small amount of unspoiled wheat that could be recovered from the ship was salvaged and eventually exported, while the grain contaminated by seawater was ground up and used for animal feed.

In 1944, the ship was built from keel to truck in only seventy-five days and launched as the EC-2 cargo ship *Edwin A. Stevens* at the Delta Shipbuilding yard in New Orleans.

CHAPTER 4

"HERCULANEAN FEATS"

On February 21, 1901, the new century was just a little more than a month old when the Pacific Mail "China steamer" *City of Rio de Janeiro*, captained by William Ward, slowly feeling her way through a dense morning fog that lay like a thick blanket on the water, struck a submerged rock off Fort Point near the mouth of San Francisco Bay.

The 3,548-ton ship, inbound from Hong Kong with a cargo of baled silk, pig iron and tin ingots, went down in less than twenty minutes. She took with her 128 people, including her captain and the U.S. consul general at Hong Kong, Rounsevelle Wildman, and his wife and children.

A grotesque reminder of one of the most appalling maritime disasters in American history, Captain Ward's body washed up near Fort Point in July 1902, seventeen months after the *City of Rio de Janeiro* went to the bottom. What could be identified as the remains of a number of other victims were still being recovered years after the ship went down.

Though several attempts were made at salvage, no trace of the ship was found, as the technology of the day didn't permit salvage at such a depth.

Among those later fêted for coming to the rescue of the survivors struggling in the wreckage-strewn water were a trio of Italian immigrants: fishermen Andrew Adami and Alberto Gibelli and Gaspare Palazzolo, captain of the fishing smack *Citta di NY*.

The *Los Angeles Herald* ran a piece claiming that the ship "had a hoodoo on her," citing an 1890 collision in Hong Kong that almost sank her; a grounding at Kagoshima, Japan, in 1895; an incident the following year

The *City of Rio de Janeiro*, built in 1878, wrecked in 1901. *Courtesy of the San Francisco Maritime NHP.*

when she almost ran out of coal in mid-Pacific; and a May 1898 collision with an unidentified freighter off the coast of Yokohama, Japan.

As could be expected, rumors circulating that she was carrying a large cache of gold and silver spurred frantic salvage attempts over the following decades, including that of a clairvoyant, one Miss A. Hatland, who, according to the October 26 edition of the *San Francisco Call*, was "the latest to come forward with 'inside' knowledge." The amazing Miss Hatland, it reported, "has hired a Crowley launch and today will go forth to find and buoy the wreck. She will carry with her an electrical device, one end of which will be dropped where the spirits told her the *Rio* rests."

The plan called for the "electrical device" to be lowered into the water and dragged along the bottom. "When the submerged wreck finder touches the *Rio*'s hull," the paper wrote, "a bell will ring on board the launch, and a division of the treasure will be a mere matter of counting it out to the stock holders."

All to no avail, however, as Miss Hatland and her "magic wand" failed to locate the wreck, much to the consternation of those who'd actually invested in her fantastic scheme.

But the following day, the *Call* wryly commented, "Miss Hatland still has faith in the spirits, but says that the tide was too strong yesterday to admit of a satisfactory test. She says that she will try again at some future date. Meanwhile, the pig iron that the spirits mistook for treasure is corroding, the raw silk turning into seaweed, and Captain Barber still believes that the *Rio* lies off Point Diablo in 60 fathoms of water."

A second attempt to find the wreck never materialized. Miss Hatland and her incredible contraption disappeared into the mists of time, and to this day, the wreck of the *City of Rio de Janeiro* lies undiscovered somewhere on the cluttered seabed near the mouth of the Golden Gate, battered and scattered by constantly shifting currents.

SEPTEMBER 8, 1923: EIGHT SHIPS LOST IN ONE DAY

Launched in Germany as the *Coblenz* in 1897, the steamer *Cuba*, captained by Charles Holland, was northbound from Panama for San Francisco with 112 people and a cargo of mahogany, silver bullion, sugar and bagged coffee aboard when she struck a reef about a quarter mile off Point Bennett on San Miguel Island in the early morning hours of September 8, 1923.

She was working up the coast when she encountered thick fog and was forced to navigate by dead reckoning for three days. To compound the situation, the ship's radio was reportedly not working, and there were no spare parts aboard to fix the problem.

After efforts to back the ship off the reef proved fruitless, passengers were loaded into the lifeboats, with everyone aboard eventually saved.

One of the ship's lifeboats was spotted and reported by the USS *Reno*, which was part of a flotilla of U.S. Navy destroyers outbound from San Francisco for San Diego on a two-day training cruise. Just a few hours later, that flotilla would be on center stage in the greatest peacetime disaster in the history of the U.S. Navy, as seven of the *Reno*'s sister ships went aground in the fog at Honda Point near the Point Arguello Light.

The "four stackers" had "conducted tactical and gunnery exercises en route, including a competitive speed run of 20 knots. Later in the day, as weather worsened, the ships formed column on the squadron leader *Delphy*," according to the report filed by the U.S. Navy's official Board of Inquiry.

At about 8:00 p.m., "the flagship broadcast an erroneous report—based on an improperly interpreted radio compass bearing—showing the squadrons position about nine miles off Point Arguello. An hour later, the destroyers turned east to enter what was thought to be the Santa Barbara Channel, though it could not be seen, owing to thick fog."

Like sleek, steel lemmings, all of Destroyer Division 33 ships and two from Destroyer Division 31—the USS *Fuller*, the USS *Woodbury*, the USS

September 8, 1923: The U.S. Navy destroyer USS *Chauncey* in the foreground on the rocks at Honda Point with the USS *Young* capsized off her stern. In the background are the USS *Woodbury* and, beyond, the USS *Fuller*. *Courtesy of the U.S. Naval History & Heritage Command Center.*

Chauncey, the USS *Young*, the USS *S.P. Lee* and the USS *Nicholas*—followed their squadron leader, the USS *Delphy*, in single file (from two hundred to five hundred yards apart) onto the rocks in just five minutes while making twenty knots. Two other destroyers were seriously damaged trying to rescue the survivors. Twenty crewmen from the USS *Young* died when she capsized, and three more were lost aboard the USS *Delphy*. The navy later estimated that the loss of the seven destroyers totaled more than $13 million.

The Navy Board affixed blame for the unprecedented event on an inaccurate navigational bearing causing the lead ship to make a wrong turn to port in the belief that she was entering the Santa Barbara Channel. Eleven officers were charged with "culpable inefficiency in the performance of their duties" and court-martialed. The commanding officer of Destroyer Squadron 11, Edward Watson, and Lieutenant Commander Donald Hunter, commanding officer of the USS *Delphy*, were found guilty, while the commanding officers of the other six ships suffered under a long-lasting cloud that darkened their future advancement in the navy.

According to maritime archaeologist and historian Robert Schwemmer, there was speculation at the time that the additional radio traffic between the ships involved in the rescue of the *Cuba*'s passengers and crew might have caused the destroyer's error in navigation by interfering with the relatively new RDF (radio direction finder) technology the doomed warships were using to navigate.

Others fixed blame for the duplicate tragedies on the September 1 tsunami that had struck Japan and, as they claimed, created a tidal wave that had traveled across the Pacific to impact the currents and wave action all along the North American West Coast at the same time the *Cuba* and the seven destroyers were wrecked.

The Devil's Jaws at Point Honda claimed another victim on May 28, 1933, when a navigational error and a thick fog combined to put the four-hundred-foot-long Japanese-flag tanker *Nippon Maru*, captained by T. Oni, on the rocks amidst the wrecks of the seven ill-fated U.S. Navy destroyers that had wrecked there a decade earlier.

Efforts to pull the ship off the rocks began almost immediately. The wreck was salvaged "in situ," but several weeks later, she slipped off the rocks and went to the bottom not far offshore.

THE *TOLO*: THE CREW ALL SAVED, WHILE RESCUERS PERISH

Laden with a deckload of stacked lumber, the schooner *Tolo* went on the rocks at South Point while working out of Caspar Creek on January 2, 1871.

According to the *Sacramento Daily Union*, "The crew was saved, but two men belonging to the mill, while endeavoring to rescue them, were drowned."

A few weeks after the wreck, the *Daily Alta California* ran an eyebrow-raising piece: "Capt. Brown, formerly master of the schooner *Tolo*, claims to have found a method by which the captains of vessels can find out the longitude and latitude they are in by observations of the rising and setting sun."

A demonstration, the paper wrote tongue-in-cheek, "was shown to our reporter last evening, and he says, although not a nautical sharp, he has no doubt the thing is a success and that he sees no reason why the same figures and explanation, drawn out a trifle, could not tell who is to be the next Governor of California."

THE *ELIZABETH*: GALLANT RESCUE ATTEMPTS FAIL

Including her master, Captain J. Herbert Colcord, eighteen people died when the ship *Elizabeth* was driven ashore by gale-force winds and lost on February 21, 1891, at Tennessee Cove, four miles from the Point Bonita Light.

The tug *Relief* went to the stricken ship's assistance but was only able to get within one hundred yards of her. A crewman aboard the tug later said, "I never saw a ship go to pieces so fast in all my life." Two brave attempts by crews of the U.S. Life-Saving Service—one by boat and the other overland—to reach the wreck were unsuccessful, the first effort costing the life of Captain Henry of the Baker's Beach Life-Saving Station.

An article in the *Daily Alta California* the day after the wreck reported, "It has been ascertained that there is really no insurance on the hull of the ship, which was valued at $75,000. The cargo was valued at $100,000…the *Elizabeth* was in Monterey Bay the day preceding the wreck, and took the inshore route up the coast, thus missing the pilots."

The ship was owned by Pendleton, Carter & Nicholas of New York. The wreck and what cargo could be salvaged were sold later at auction for $555.

THE *SEA NYMPH*: THE SHIP AND ONE MAN LOST

Heavy fog was blamed for the May 4, 1861 loss of the medium clipper *Sea Nymph* on the rocks of Three Mile Beach, just a few miles north of Point Reyes. Built in 1853, she had made four voyages between New York and San Francisco before she was lost.

The wreck and her cargo, alone valued at $250,000, were sold at auction in San Francisco for $6,650. The *Daily Alta California* of May 7, 1861, reported, "When she struck the Captain commenced firing signal guns of distress, and in about an hour, persons came to the beach; in the meantime, the masts had been cut away and drifted ashore with the sails."

A "kite" was sent ashore with spun yarn attached that was used to gradually increase the size of the line at intervals. Eventually, a large hawser connected the ship with a sturdy pole on the hillside to keep the line out of the pounding surf.

Before and after the light at Point Reyes was commissioned in 1870, scores of ships met their fates on the jagged rocks almost three hundred feet below. This image was taken by the noted English-born nature photographer Eadweard Muybridge a year after the lighthouse was built. *Courtesy of the U.S. Coast Guard.*

A canvas sling was rigged to run along the hawser, and by midnight, only seven crewmen remained on board the *Sea Nymph*, all of whom were rescued with the exception of one man, steward Henry Harris.

THE *NORTHERNER*: A MOUNTAIN MAN
TO THE RESCUE

Struggling to maintain headway in a raging gale, the wooden Pacific Mail side-wheeler *Northerner* struck an unmarked and uncharted submerged rock near Blunts Reef, about twenty miles south of Humboldt Bay, on January 5, 1860.

The ship was built in 1847 in New York by William H. Brown & Co. and was on a passage from San Francisco to the Columbia River and Puget Sound.

Among the cargo were two horses that survived and forty-eight sacks of U.S. Mail that were recovered. Some $14,000 in Wells, Fargo & Co. gold was lost, as were the lives of thirty-eight passengers and crewmen.

The *Northerner*'s master, Captain William Dall, was the last to leave the wrecked ship and was praised for his "gallant" efforts to save the ship and as many passengers and crew as possible.

Among the lost was Francis Bloomfield, son of the bishop of London, who'd arrived in San Francisco via Panama just a week before the wreck. The young adventurer was "going up the coast to see a region new to him," wrote the *Sacramento Daily Union*. Bodies and debris from the ship reportedly washed ashore for weeks after the wreck, but Bloomfield's body was never recovered.

The people of the small nearby town of Centerville provided food and shelter for the survivors of the wreck, while the remains of the victims that could be recovered were buried in a mass grave near the beach that is still marked by the Centerville Beach Cross.

The story is told of the self-described mountain man, elk-horn chair maker and Centerville resident Seth Kinman responding to the *Northerner*'s distress signals by tethering himself to a rock and wading into the pounding surf to rescue more than a dozen exhausted and dazed survivors.

Hailed as a hero, Kinman was presented with a leather-bound Bible and a specially printed ticket giving him free lifetime passage on Pacific Mail steamships.

The *Eureka*: A "Sturdy Crew of Lifesavers"

The North Pacific Steamship Company's steamer *Eureka* was bound from San Francisco to Ventura when she was struck by a big sea and capsized off Point Bonita on January 8, 1915.

The *Sausalito News* reported, "She had a heavy list which made her susceptible to the heavy sea. Captain Ingersoll, keeper of the Point Bonita Lighthouse, sent out word of her condition. Captain Nutter and his sturdy crew of lifesavers kept up their excellent reputation as lifesavers, performing herculanean feats."

The paper also lauded the officers and men of the nearby U.S. Coast Artillery garrison at Fort Barry, who assisted in the rescue and care of the shipwrecked crew.

The 142-foot-long, 484-ton *Eureka* was said to be the largest and fastest steam schooner built up to that time. Her first mate, James Bolger, was the only crewman lost in the wreck. His body was never recovered.

The USS *Milwaukee*: An Unequal Trade-Off

On January 13, 1917, the protected cruiser USS *Milwaukee* went ashore broadside on Samoa Beach while attempting to salvage the submarine USS *H-3*, which had run aground a month earlier.

The 426-foot-long, 9,700-ton *Milwaukee* had been launched at the Union Iron Works shipyard in San Francisco in 1906.

The crew reached shore safely, but attempts to salvage the ship were unsuccessful. Salvagers built a rail-equipped pier out to the wreck to facilitate the removal of the ship's guns and other equipment.

Salvors built a railroad trestle to haul away the guns, ammunition, stores and equipment they were able to remove from the armored cruiser USS *Milwaukee* after she went aground on Samoa Beach. *Courtesy of the Special Collections Library, Humboldt State University.*

The *Milwaukee* was decommissioned the following March, broke up in a November 1918 storm and was officially struck from the navy's list of active duty vessels in June 1919. What was left of her hulk was sold two months later.

The *H-3* was eventually salvaged when the Mercer-Fraser Company, a lumber company based in nearby Eureka, underbid a competitor to get the job. Workers then lifted the 467-ton submarine onto giant log rollers and moved it overland to the waters of nearby Humboldt Bay, where she was refloated.

THE *MARY STUART*: "NO BLAME OF ANY KIND"

Bound for Mazatlan with sixty passengers and a cargo of quicksilver, the brig *Mary Stuart*, captained by Charles Thompson, was wrecked after she went ashore before dawn on June 20, 1851, at Point Ano Nuevo, about forty miles south of the Golden Gate.

The day after the wreck, the *Daily Alta California* reported that "Mr. McDonald owner of the Mary Stuart…has called upon us and suggested us to state in his own name and that of the passengers, of the vessel that no blame of any kind is attributable to the master for the unfortunate occurrence."

Captain Thompson, said McDonald, "managed to get her inside the bar, and got a rope ashore by which means he saved the passengers at the risk of his own life. The scene was a terrible one as is described by an eye witness, there being about sixty passengers on board and among them a number of females."

Very few wrecks have occurred, the paper said, "where the danger was so imminent as in this case without anything more serious happening."

ALBERT AND EDWARD: "CLINGING TO THE SHROUDS"

Five crewmen aboard the schooner *Albert and Edward* died when the two-master capsized and was wrecked on the evening of April 18, 1875, while crossing the Humboldt Bar.

Owned by Higgins & Clark of San Francisco, the *Albert and Edward* had discharged her ballast at sea when a heavy sea struck her, demolishing the wheel and sending two men overboard. The schooner broached to, and the next heavy sea capsized her.

According to the *Daily Alta California*, the steam tug *Mary Ann* was close by and succeeded in saving one of the two men.

As the ship listed and started to go under, the paper reported, "Captain Ericson, the mate, the cook and one seaman succeeded in saving themselves for a time by clinging to the shrouds."

The schooner soon turned turtle and drifted southward, bottom up, with four men clinging to the hull. Several attempts were made by the crew of the *Mary Ann* to rescue the men.

A line was thrown over the vessel several times, but either because of fright, exhaustion or some other cause, the men failed to take hold and be pulled to safety. When dawn came, the pair was gone, and within a day, the ship had gone to pieces.

The *Aimer*, the *Reporter* and the *Gipsy*: Strange Lights Beckon

On June 26, 1871, the schooner *Aimer* went aground on Ocean Beach close to the Ocean Side House near the mouth of the Golden Gate. She was inbound from Coos Bay and laden with 140 tons of coal, thirty-five thousand board feet of lumber and a few dozen cords of firewood.

According to the *Daily Alta California*, "There was a dense fog outside at the time, and a strong southerly current. A light at the Ocean Side House was mistaken for [Point Bonita] light, and the captain, keeping the vessel away for what he supposed was the entrance to the harbor, in a short time found himself in the breakers." Both her anchors were let go, but neither would hold, and the *Aimer* went ashore.

Almost six weeks of work went into the effort to pull her off. They were almost met with success, but all came to naught when the hawsers holding her to a salvage tug parted and she went ashore for the second time to be pounded to kindling in the surf—"a new attraction is thus open to visitors to the Cliff House and beach," the paper said.

The Cliff House played host to another ill-illumined shipwreck when the three-masted schooner *Reporter* was wrecked on March 13, 1902, on the beach a little less than a mile below the iconic structure.

The victim of a misread signal lamp, the steam schooner *Gipsy* was beaten to pieces in the surf near Monterey Bay. *Courtesy of the Pacific Grove Museum of Natural History.*

With an uninsured cargo of 400,000 board feet of lumber, laths and shakes and six days out of Grays Harbor, the schooner came to grief when her master, Captain Adolph Hansen, repeated the *Aimer*'s fatal error of three decades before and mistook "a strange light" in the vicinity of the Cliff House for the Point Bonita Light.

The *San Francisco Call* wrote that the ship went aground within a few yards of the partially buried hulk of the *King Philip*, which was lost there in 1878, "…within sight of the cove where the little *Neptune* drove upon the sands. All day the wreck was the prize show of the year. Thousands visited the scene, and not even the biting wind and sudden squalls could drive them away."

The wreck was such a popular attraction, the paper observed, that it "proved to be a financial benefit to the Market Street Railway, the waffle man, the peanut vendor and the saloon men on the beach." The *Reporter* was considered one of the fastest schooners in the coastal lumber trade and was owned by the E.K. Wood Lumber Company.

Another ship lured to her doom by a "strange light," the *Gipsy* was lost in what has to be one of the most unique tales of shipwreck ever told.

Sailing under the Pacific Coast Steamship Company house flag, the wooden steam schooner went on the rocks off McAbee's Beach in Monterey Bay, near what is now Cannery Row, on September 27, 1905.

The blame for the loss of the ship was placed on, of all things, sewer maintenance.

According to the wreck report filed by her master, Captain Thomas Boyd, "It is customary for the ship's agent to hang a red lantern on the wharf to direct the steamer to the landing, but on the night of the wreck, the man on watch mistook a red lantern hung over an open sewer under repair for the signal, and the vessel ran upon a reef."

The ship and her cargo, valued at $22,500, were a total loss. All hands aboard, including the undoubtedly chagrined and mercifully unnamed "man on watch," were saved.

The *Gipsy*—built in 1868 and the oldest ship in the PCSC fleet—had plied the route between San Francisco and Monterey for fifteen years with such mundane regularity that she was fondly nicknamed "Old Perpetual Motion."

THE *CITY OF NEW YORK*: ROCKETS AND SIGNAL GUNS

Such was the magnitude of her loss that the story of the wreck of the screw steamer *City of New York* took up the entire front page of the October 26, 1893 edition of the *San Francisco Call*, as well as several other papers.

The previous day, the Pacific Mail Steamship Company (PMSC) screw steamer was outbound from San Francisco for China with Captain Frank Johnston in command and pilot George Johnson at the helm to steer her through the Golden Gate. Aboard were 133 Chinese passengers and 104 crewmen.

A heavy fog—low and thick—suddenly rolled in, blanketing the ship's course. The *San Francisco Call* reported that shortly thereafter, "the telephone-bell in the exchange rang at 4:45 and Keeper John Hyslop at the association's station sent a message that an unknown vessel was on the rocks near Point Bonita. Rockets had been sent up and signal-guns were booming."

Fortunately, there were no casualties in the wreck. The *City of New York*'s cargo was valued at almost $100,000, with the manifest including such varied items as ginseng, flour, pearl barley, dried seaweed, shrimp shells, apples, beans, ivory, potatoes, onions, lard, confectionary and canned fruit and salmon, most shipped by Chinese merchants and later salvaged. Also aboard were several dozen sacks of U.S. Mail and a little more than $1 million in Mexican dollars, gold dust and other gold coins, about half of which was eventually recovered.

The wreck of the *City of New York* was eventually sold for scrapping to Captain Thomas Whitelaw, the legendary San Francisco–based salvage master.

Efforts to salvage what could be removed from the hulk continued until January 1895, when the salvage ship *Samson*, working the wreck, was caught in a sudden southeast gale and lost along with her four-man crew on the same rocks that claimed the *City of New York*.

The *Colombia*, the *Chateau Palmer* and the *Dorothy Wintermote*: Free for the Taking

At 8:00 a.m. on July 14, 1896, the Pacific Mail steamship *Colombia*, from Acapulco for San Francisco, went ashore bow-on in a heavy fog on the rocks near Pigeon Point, a rocky promontory about five miles from Pescadero. The *Los Angeles Herald* wrote that the steamer "was nearer the shore than her skipper realized, and before her course could be altered, those on board could hear the rocks scraping her keel."

She went ashore just below the Pigeon Point Lighthouse, about one hundred yards from shore close to where the *Hellespont* was wrecked in 1868. The 3,616-ton *Colombia* had thirty-six cabin and twenty-six steerage passengers and a crew of ninety men aboard when she was wrecked. All were saved.

The official wreck report concluded that the mishap was caused by a combination of heavy fog and mistaken bearings.

The *Colombia*'s cargo manifest read like a Sears Roebuck catalogue: cases of unbleached cotton, dolls, coffee grinders, barbed wire, licorice, axes, tin ware, whiskey, pick handles, baby carriages, nuts and washers, toothpicks, wooden toys, hinges, pencil lead, pianos, bar soap, sewing machines, solder, boot blacking, ladies' hosiery, tropical fruit, house paint and much more.

After the *Colombia*'s wreck, according to one newspaper account, huge crowds of sightseers flocked to Pigeon Point to view the doomed steamer. Gleeful children entertained themselves by recovering armfuls of limes, mangoes and toys that bobbed ashore, while, over the following weeks, the nearby town of Pescadero reportedly had a number of houses that mysteriously sported gleaming coats of fresh white paint.

It wasn't just any cargo that washed ashore when the *Chateau Palmer* was transformed into a total wreck after being driven ashore by a strong northwest blow and heavy swells about five hundred yards west of Fort Point.

According to the *Sacramento Daily Union* of May 7, 1856, the ship "can be almost approached on foot at extreme low water, but at high water she is being continually washed over. The beach is strewed with pieces of the wreck, and several barrels of liquor have washed ashore, which have speedily been taken care of by those at work."

The previous day, the paper had reported, "A large number of ladies and gentlemen walked out to the spot, and as the day was remarkably clear and pleasant, they had a fine view of the vessel. Such as wished it were favored with a glass of excellent claret, a cask of which had been washed ashore, and was tapped for the general benefit of the visitors."

Years later, the *Ukiah Republican Press* reported that after the October 20, 1938 wreck of the lumber steamer *Dorothy Wintermote* at the mouth of the Gualala River, "enough coffee to last the residents of Mendocino County for some time washed ashore."

The 2,016-ton ship, built as the *Lake Cayuga* in 1918, was carrying a cargo of general merchandise, including twenty tons of vacuum-packed Hill's Bros. "Red Can" coffee packed in cardboard cartons that disintegrated when they spilled from the hold.

Within hours, two-, four- and fifteen-pound cans of coffee, somewhat battered in the surf, covered the beach for more than half a mile, with some entrepreneurial souls reportedly selling much of what they salvaged to local general stores and markets.

The *Corinthian*: "Not Sufficiently Powerful"

Just two months after the loss of the *Newsboy* at the same spot, young Andrew McCarrey, a student at the University of California who had shipped aboard as the cook's helper, was one of the two men lost when the gasoline schooner *Corinthian* was wrecked on the Humboldt Bar on June 11, 1906.

The *San Francisco Call* wrote that "the wreck was caused by the fact that the bar was rough and the vessel was not sufficiently powerful to make headway and escape the rollers."

The two-masted, white-hulled schooner *Corinthian*. Two men died when she was wrecked on the Humboldt Bar near Eureka on June 12, 1906. *Courtesy of the San Francisco Maritime NHP.*

The other man lost was Ole Carlson, who drowned in the breakers when he was washed overboard. When the *Corinthian* struck, her deckload of lumber went into the water, severely injuring two men who were trying to save the men still aboard. Her master, Captain Atwater, was the last to leave the ship, having spent the entire night after the schooner went ashore clinging to the rigging with the surf breaking over him.

THE *LAMMERMOOR*: ONE OF THE MOST BEAUTIFUL IRON CLIPPERS

Named for the locale in a story by Sir Walter Scott, the *Lammermoor* was wrecked on June 27, 1882, in heavy weather about a half mile south of Bodega Bay.

Considered one of the most beautiful and "splendid" iron clippers ever built, the three-masted extreme clipper sailed under the Red Duster of Britain's Mercantile Marine and was lost inbound for San Francisco from Sydney, Australia.

Several members of the crew told eager reporters that "the ship at the time she stuck was booming along under full sail and leading wind" and that "there was no lookout on duty at the time."

The naval court of inquiry called by the British Consul to investigate the ship's loss found that the ship's master, Captain Gathrie, bore sole responsibility for the wreck. The court found that he had been seventy-five miles off course and had failed to take soundings and alter the course of the ship.

Gathrie's certificate was suspended for six months, and what was left of the *Lammermoor* and her cargo later fetched all of $830 at auction.

THE *ERIN'S STAR*: A "FINE VESSEL SACRIFICED"

The bark *Erin's Star* and her cargo of steel rails were lost when she went aground in a thick fog off Point Reyes.

"It is not improbable that the wreck might be attributed to negligence on the part of the keepers of the fog whistle on Point Reyes," opined the *Daily Alta California* a few days after the September 13, 1881 wreck.

According to the statements of two shipmasters who submitted a complaint to the U.S. Lighthouse Board, "the fog whistle was not blowing…Masters rely

Station keeper Christopher Hunt and the crew of the Point Reyes U.S. Life-Saving Station pose for a formal portrait. Hunt commanded the station from 1907 to 1915. Established in 1890, the original station was located on desolate and exposed Great Beach near the east head of Point Reyes. *Courtesy of the Golden Gate NRA.*

on these warnings, and it is better to remove them altogether if they cannot be properly attended to."

The *Erin's Star*'s master, the paper continued, "might have been warned in time by the whistle, as it is plainly stated that it can plainly be heard a distance of twelve miles in moderate weather. As the matter stands, a fine vessel and a valuable cargo are sacrificed, and the matter calls for a most rigid official investigation."

The USS *Makassar Strait*, the USS *George A. Johnson* and the *La Janelle*: Dying on Their Own Terms

The war-weary, Casablanca-class escort aircraft carrier USS *Makassar Strait* spent almost fifteen years in the Pacific Reserve Fleet near Tacoma, Washington, before the navy decided to use her as a remote-controlled target ship.

In April 1961, while under tow to San Clemente Island, the towline parted and the "jeep" carrier went aground on San Nicholas Island. The years passed, and plans to break up the ship in situ remained unfulfilled.

The ship had been commissioned in 1944 and received two battle stars for her World War II service in the Southwest Pacific.

A veteran of combat action in both the Atlantic and Pacific Theaters during World War II, the three-hundred-foot-long Rudderow-class destroyer escort USS *George A. Johnson* was used to train naval reservists before she was placed in the fleet reserve at Mare Island in 1957.

Sold for scrapping to the National Metals Co., she was being towed south to the breaker's yard on Terminal Island at the Port of Los Angeles when she parted her towline and went ashore at Pacifica on October 12, 1966. She was broken up in place when it was determined that the cost of refloating her would exceed her scrap value.

The 465-foot-long liner *La Janelle*—launched as the *Borinquen* in 1930 at the Bethlehem yard in Bath, Maine—was wrecked at Port Hueneme at the end of a varied career that saw her serve at different times as an immigrant ship, passenger and cruise ship and World War II military transport.

She went ashore on April 13, 1970, when her chains parted in gale-force winds and heavy swells while anchored offshore to avoid expensive dock fees. Some sources claim the Western Shipping Company, the *La Janelle*'s last owners, had sailed her to Hueneme, where they intended to sell her. Other accounts say that plans were underway to make her a floating restaurant/casino, while still others claim she was to be sold to an Indonesian shipping firm for conversion to a freighter. However, none of the plans ever materialized.

Abandoned as a total loss, the *La Janelle* was stripped of any useful equipment and later transformed into an extension of the port's breakwater.

AFTERWORD

The number of ships lost on California's coast has diminished considerably over the past fifty years as advanced shipbuilding techniques, enhanced safety standards, crew licensing and training, highly detailed charts, radar and satellite navigation have significantly reduced the chance of mishap, either natural or man-made.

But all of that proved of little use to the 531-foot, 14,412-ton bulk carrier *Pacbaroness*, which foundered after a collision in heavy seas and fog with the Korean-flag car carrier *Atlantic Wing* on the morning of September 2, 1987.

With a 12-foot gash in her starboard side, the Japanese-built ship, equipped with the most modern navigational and radar equipment, went down in more than 1,400 feet of water about ten miles southwest of Point Conception after attempts to tow her to safety failed.

She was carrying a cargo of 21,000 metric tons of finely powdered copper concentrate, 339,360 gallons of fuel oil and 10,015 gallons of lubricating oil when she sank. The initial U.S. Coast Guard investigation indicated that approximately 20,000 gallons of oil had spilled from the sunken wreck and that some of her cargo of copper concentrate escaped into the water from her breached holds.

Following the sinking, a slick formed in the vicinity of the wreck site that was one and a half miles long and a half mile wide. A large quantity of oil continued to bubble to the surface for several days after the *Pac Baroness* went down.

An attempt to tow the bulk carrier *Pacbaroness* to safety proved futile after her September 21, 1987 collision with a Korean-flag auto carrier near Point Conception. *Courtesy of Glenn Allen and Robert V. Schwemmer.*

Human fallibility, "eccentric" fog, contrary currents, violent storms, collisions, fire, explosions, the treacherous Humboldt River Bar and the silent hazards of Point Arena, the Farallons, Point Reyes, Ocean Beach and so many others have each doomed their own fair share of the wrecks that pepper the state's rugged, forbidding shoreline.

No one knows the name of the first ship to come to grief on the California coast, nor can anyone predict the name of the next. This continues to be, then, the middle of a long, poignant—and sometimes inspiring—story that has no known beginning and no forecasted end.

What is known, though, is that the stories told in this book serve as sobering reminders that the Golden State's shore has always been and always will be a very ruggedly beautiful but unforgiving place.

A CHRONOLOGY OF LOSSES

The catalogue below is hardly comprehensive but is meant to illustrate the chronological and geographic scope of the large number of documented wrecks that litter the coastline of Upper and Lower California. While many locales have been dubbed the maritime "graveyard" of their respective Pacific and Atlantic regions, few can doubt that the following list of ships—each with its own story to tell—shows that California can unquestionably submit a valid claim to such a melancholy title.

1540—*Trinidad*, galleon, wrecked near San Diego

1582—*Santa Marta*, galleon, wrecked on Santa Catalina Island

November ___, 1595—*San Agustin*, galleon, wrecked at Point Reyes

1641—*Nuestra Senora de Ayuda*, galleon, lost on Santa Catalina Island

1754—*San Sebastian*, galleon, lost on Santa Catalina Island

1797—*San Carlos*, ship, wrecked in San Francisco Bay

1823—*Neriede*, ship, lost on the California coast

Crewmen struggle aloft to keep an unnamed dismasted sixteenth-century Spanish galleon from disaster. *Author's collection.*

December 25, 1828—*Danube*, brigantine, lost at Point Fermin

December 21, 1834—*Natalia*, brig, ashore and wrecked in Monterey Bay

January 7, 1836—*Peor Es Nada*, schooner, wrecked at the Golden Gate

November 19, 1836—*Commodore Rodgers*, ship, lost at Monterey Bay

October 27, 1841—*Ayachuco*, brig, wrecked at Drake's Bay

July 27, 1845—*Star of the West*, schooner, lost at Point Lobos

February 26, 1846—*Fama*, schooner, ashore and wrecked near Goleta

November 8, 1847—*Francisca*, brig, wrecked at Santa Barbara

February 14, 1848—*Elizabeth*, brig, ashore and wrecked at Santa Barbara

1849—*Helena*, ship, wrecked at Bodega Bay

May __, 1849—*Flora*, sloop, sank in San Francisco Bay

August 24, 1849—USS *Edith*, bark-rigged steamer, wrecked at Point Conception

November 20, 1849—*Tonquin*, ship, lost on Whalesman Shoal

November 20, 1849—*Crown Princess*, ship, wrecked on Devil's Point

December 16, 1849—*Thomas H. Benton*, brig, wrecked on Angel Island

December 17, 1849—*Mary Jane*, schooner, ashore and wrecked at Timm's Point

January 29, 1850—*Colonel Cross*, steamship, wrecked off Yerba Buena

March 19, 1850—*Caroline Amelia*, bark, wrecked on Mile Rock

April __, 1850—*Paragon*, schooner, wrecked at Point St. George

June 12, 1850—*Robert Henderson*, bark, ashore and wrecked on Ocean Beach

June 26, 1850—*Utica*, ship, burned and sunk in San Francisco Bay

July 26, 1850—*Frolic*, clipper brig, ashore and wrecked on the Mendocino coast

August 4, 1850—*Marshall*, brig, aground and lost at Bodega Bay

October 25, 1850—*Patuxent*, schooner, aground and lost at Trinidad Bay

November 19, 1850—*Glouchester*, bark, capsized and sank in San Francisco Bay

December 16, 1850—*Mersey*, bark, wrecked at the Golden Gate

January 7, 1851—*Brutus*, brig, ashore between San Ramon and Salinas

March __, 1851—*Susan Wardwell*, schooner, lost on the Humboldt Bar

March __, 1851—*Zachary Johnson*, schooner, wrecked at Trinidad

March __, 1851—*Chesapeake*, schooner, wrecked at Trinidad

March 3, 1851—*Santa Clara*, steamship, burned out in San Francisco Bay

May 6, 1851—*Commodore Preble*, steamer, wrecked at Humboldt Bay

June 20, 1851—*Mary Stuart*, brig, wrecked at Point Ano Nuevo

July 2, 1851—*Union*, steamer, wrecked at Punta Beja, Baja California

August 3, 1851—*Tagus*, ship, ashore four miles north of the Golden Gate

August 19, 1851—*J. Sarkie*, bark, ashore and wrecked at Point Lobos

November 25, 1851—*Cornelius W. Lawrence*, revenue cutter, lost at Ocean Beach

December 13, 1851—*Fanny*, pilot schooner, lost at Ballast Point, San Diego

December 30, 1851—*New England*, bark, wrecked on Angel Island

January 25, 1852—*Sea Gull*, steamer, ashore and lost at Humboldt Bay

February 10, 1852—*Burnea Dea*, schooner, lost on the Humboldt Bar

May 27, 1852—*John Clifford*, brig, wrecked on the Humboldt Bar

June 7, 1852—*Cornwallis*, bark, wrecked on the Humboldt Bar

June 11, 1852—*Traveler*, schooner, burned and sank at Santa Cruz

July 14, 1852—*Oxford*, ship, wrecked at Tomales Bay

August 16, 1852—*Pioneer*, steamer, lost at St. Simon's Bay, Baja California

August 23, 1852—*Petersburg*, brig, wrecked north of Point Bonita

November __, 1852—*Samoset*, ship, wrecked at Fort Point

November 29, 1852—*Sheriff*, schooner, sank at Kent's Point

December 1, 1852—*Samoset*, ship, wrecked at Fort Point

1853—*Galileo*, ship, foundered at Santa Rosa Island

January __, 1853—*Mary*, schooner, lost on the Bolinas Bar

January 6, 1853—*Sea Witch*, pilot schooner, wrecked on Arch Rock

January 7, 1853—*Aberdeen*, ship, aground and wrecked near Fort Point

March 6, 1853—*Tennessee*, steamer, lost at Tennessee Cove

April 9, 1853—*Samuel S. Lewis*, steamer, wrecked on Duxbury Reef

May 27, 1853—*Arispe*, steamer, wrecked near Fort Ros

June 6, 1853—*Carrier Pigeon*, ship, ashore and wrecked at Santa Cruz

June 24, 1853—*Sea Bird*, salvage steamer, wrecked at Pigeon Point

June 24, 1853—*America*, ship, wrecked at Crescent City

October 16, 1853—*Independence*, steamer, wrecked off Baja California

December 1, 1853—*Winfield Scott*, steamer, wrecked on Anacapa Island

December 8, 1853—*San Francisco*, ship, wrecked at Point Bonita

December 10, 1853—*Mexican*, schooner, lost on the Humboldt Bar

1854—*W.T. Wheaton*, schooner, wrecked south of Point Sur

February __, 1854—*San Mateo*, schooner, foundered off the coast of Northern California

February 8, 1854—*San Francisco*, ship, wrecked at Point Bonita

April 21, 1854—*Walter Claxton*, bark, wrecked near Mendocino

The 115-foot-tall Pigeon Point Lighthouse, with a lens producing a light of 500,000 candlepower, was built in 1872 to guide ships approaching San Francisco Bay from the south. *Courtesy of the U.S. Coast Guard.*

April 22, 1854—*Golden Fleece*, ship, foundered near the Golden Gate

May 23, 1854—*Donna Maria*, schooner, ashore and wrecked near Fort Ross

May 27, 1854—*Arispe*, steamer, wrecked north of Fort Ross

October 1, 1854—*Yankee Blade*, steamer, wrecked near Point Bonita

February __, 1855—*Piedmont*, schooner, wrecked on the Humboldt Bar

December 6, 1855—*La Paz*, ship, wrecked at Big River

December 6, 1855—*North Bend*, hermaphrodite brig, wrecked at Big River

December 6, 1855—*Kingsbury*, brig, wrecked at Big River

December 11, 1855—*Harriet*, schooner, wrecked at Mendocino

January 1, 1856—*Isabelita Heyne*, bark, ashore and wrecked south of Half Moon Bay

January 14, 1856—*Eliza Thornton*, schooner, wrecked at Santa Barbara

February 5, 1856—*Godle Geoch* (possibly *Gold Beach*), schooner, wrecked at Klamath

May 1, 1856—*Chateau Palmer*, ship, lost at the Golden Gate

May 17, 1856—*Toronto*, schooner, lost on the Humboldt Bar

February 8, 1857—*Lafayette*, sloop, ashore and wrecked at Fort Point

May 7, 1857—*Dancing Feather*, pilot schooner, wrecked near Point Bonita

November 1, 1857—*J.B. Brown*, schooner, ashore and lost at the Noyo River

January 10, 1858—*Charles & Edward*, schooner, ashore and wrecked at Point Arena

February 21, 1858—*Judson*, schooner, wrecked at Albion

March 15, 1858—*Maxhaul*, schooner, wrecked at San Francisquito Creek

May 1, 1858—*Zenobia*, ship, wrecked at Point Bonita

October 2, 1858—*Lovely Flora*, schooner, wrecked at San Diego

October 2, 1858—*Plutus*, schooner, ashore and wrecked at San Diego

October 13, 1858—*San Buenaventura*, sloop, foundered off Santa Cruz Island

October 16, 1858—*General Cushing*, ship, aground and wrecked at Fort Point

November 10, 1858—*Lucas*, ship, wrecked on South Farallon Island

December 11, 1858—*Iwanowna*, bark, lost on the Humboldt Bar

December 19, 1858—*J.M. Ryerson*, schooner, wrecked at Humboldt

1859—*Swiss Boy*, brig, wrecked at Humboldt

February __, 1859—*Margaret Tyson*, schooner, disappeared after clearing the Golden Gate

March __, 1859—*America*, bark, wrecked at Humboldt

March __, 1859—*Success*, bark, lost on the Humboldt Bar

March __, 1859—*Halcyon*, brig, lost at Mendocino

March 21, 1859—*Exact*, schooner, ashore and wrecked at Crescent City

March 30, 1859—*Ellen H. Wood*, brig, wrecked at Salt Point

June 29, 1859—*Julia Castner*, bark, capsized and ashore south of the Golden Gate

July __, 1859—*Plutus*, schooner, wrecked near San Diego

August __, 1859—*Forest Monarch*, ship, foundered off the coast of Northern California

August 4, 1859—*Marshall*, brig, ashore and wrecked near Bodega

September 6, 1859—*Mary F. Slade*, bark, wrecked at Cape Mendocino

December 31, 1859—*Susanita*, schooner, lost at Fort Point

January 5, 1860—*Northerner*, steamer, wrecked at Blunt's Reef

March 28, 1860—*Josefa*, schooner, foundered off the coast of Southern California

October 14, 1860—*Granada*, steamer, wrecked near Fort Point

November 16, 1860—*Eliza P. Adams*, schooner, capsized and lost off Point Bonita

1861—*European*, ship, wrecked at Tomales Bay

1861—*Cuffey's Cove*, schooner, lost at Cuffey's Cove

February 20, 1861—*Unknown*, bark, lost off Point Pedro

March 3, 1861—*Acadia*, bark, ashore and wrecked at Trinidad

May 4, 1861—*Sea Nymph*, ship, wrecked north of Point Reyes

June 26, 1861—*Palestine*, ship, lost on the San Francisco Bar

August 1, 1861—*Cleopatra*, bark, burned and sank off Cape San Lucas, Baja California

October __, 1861—*European*, schooner, lost at Tomales Bay

November 1, 1861—*Marin*, schooner, wrecked at Tomales Bay

November 4, 1861—*Salinas*, steamer, ashore and lost in Monterey Bay

November 16, 1861—*Jennie Reed*, schooner, lost near Bodega

November 23, 1861—*Maria*, schooner, wrecked at Fort Point

December __, 1861—*Bianca*, schooner, ashore and wrecked at Salt Point

1862—*C.W. Gunnel*, schooner, wrecked at Point Arena

January __, 1862—*Elfin A. Kniper*, schooner, wrecked at Half Moon Bay

January 1, 1862—*Noonday*, ship, wrecked near the Farallon Islands

January 29, 1862—*Flying Dragon*, ship, wrecked on Arch Rock

March 3, 1862—*Polynesia*, ship, burned and wrecked in San Francisco Bay

October 7, 1862—*Maryland*, schooner, wrecked on the rocks at Bowen's Landing

November __, 1862—*Constantine*, schooner, wrecked at Cuffey's Cove

December __, 1862—*C.W. Gunnel*, schooner, ashore and lost at Point Arena

December __, 1862—*H.T. Clay*, schooner, wrecked at the Noyo River

December 27, 1862—*Sovereign*, schooner, wrecked at Navarro

1863—*Frances Helen*, schooner, wrecked at Bell's Creek

1863—*Maggie Johnston*, schooner, lost at Half Moon Bay

January 1, 1863—*Noonday*, ship, lost off North Farallon Island

January 8, 1863—*F.W. Bailey*, schooner, lost at Point Lobos

January 28, 1863—*Aeolus*, schooner, wrecked on the Humboldt Bar

February 13, 1863—*J.R. Whiting*, schooner, lost at Noyo River

February 17, 1863—*Alcyone*, schooner, capsized and lost at the Noyo River

February 17, 1863—*Far West*, schooner, stranded and wrecked at Russian Gulch

February 17, 1863—*Quoddy Belle*, schooner, ashore and lost at Navarro

February 17, 1863—*Beeswing*, schooner, lost on the San Francisco Bar

February 18, 1863—*Relief*, pilot schooner, wrecked on the San Francisco Bar

April __, 1863—*Frances Helen*, schooner, wrecked at Bell's Creek

April 23, 1863—*Hyack*, bark, wrecked off Cape Mendocino

April 27, 1863—*Ada Hancock*, steam tug, lost at Wilmington after explosion

May __, 1863—*Eagle*, schooner, wrecked at Russian Gulch

May 18, 1863—*Walcott*, brig, lost at Bowen's Landing

May 21, 1863—*Galveston*, brig, ashore and wrecked at Kent's Point

September 23, 1863—*Julius Pringle*, ship, wrecked at Monterey

September 26, 1863—*Novik*, Russian screw corvette, wrecked north of Point Reyes

October 6, 1863—*Frances Ellen*, schooner, wrecked at Little River

November 15, 1863—*Aquila*, ship, sank in San Francisco Bay

November 16, 1863—*Isca*, schooner, wrecked in San Francisco Bay

December 30, 1863—*Dashaway*, schooner, wrecked south of Cape Mendocino

January 12, 1864—*Pride of the Sea*, brig, wrecked south of Santa Barbara

January 29, 1864—*Jenny Ford*, schooner, wrecked near Point Diablo

July 10, 1864—*Elizabeth Buckley*, schooner, ashore and wrecked at Point Arena

November 14, 1864—*Hartford*, bark, ashore and wrecked at Humboldt Bay

November 24, 1864—*Sagamore*, schooner, lost off Point Pinole

December 19, 1864—*H.J. Murdock*, schooner, stranded and lost at the Noyo River

1865—*Storm Cloud*, schooner, ashore and lost at Mendocino

January 4, 1865—*Ann Perry*, bark, ashore and wrecked south of the Cliff House

January 16, 1865—*Sir John Franklin*, ship, aground and wrecked at Middle Point

February 5, 1865—*Charlotte*, schooner, lost on the Klamath Bar

March 10, 1865—*Cabot*, brig, sunk at Mendocino

May 14, 1865—*Amazon*, schooner, ashore and wrecked at the Cliff House

June 16, 1865—*Kate Blakiston*, schooner, capsized and sank in San Francisco Bay

July 30, 1865—*Brother Jonathan*, steamer, wrecked off Crescent City

November 11, 1865—*Sarah Louise*, schooner, ashore and wrecked north of Tennessee Cove

November 13, 1865—*Falmouth*, schooner, ashore and wrecked below Gharkey's Wharf

November 17, 1865—*Storm Cloud*, schooner, wrecked at Mendocino

November 17, 1865—*Helen*, schooner, ashore and lost at Point Arena

November 17, 1865—*Metis*, schooner, wrecked at Caspar

November 17, 1865—*Golden State*, schooner, lost at Mendocino

January __, 1866—*Ella Frances*, bark, abandoned and sunk off Northern California

April 15, 1866—*Labouchere*, bark-rigged steamer, wrecked near Point Reyes

April 22, 1866—*Elizabeth Owens*, schooner, lost on the Seal Rocks below the Cliff House

April 30, 1866—*Amelia Francis*, sloop, burned and sunk off San Pablo Point

July 26, 1866—*Sacramento*, schooner, sank off Benicia

October __, 1866—*Glenarm*, schooner, wrecked at the Russian River

November 24, 1866—*Coya*, bark, lost near Pigeon Point

February 3, 1867—*Schah Jehan*, ship, wrecked at Point Lobos

February 21, 1867—*Buenos Dias*, schooner, capsized and lost at Red Rock

April 11, 1867—*Sine Johnson*, schooner, lost near the Navarro River

April 11, 1867—*Caleb Curtis*, pilot schooner, lost on the San Francisco Bar

April 12, 1867—*Nahumkeag*, bark, wrecked at Drake's Bay

July 26, 1867—*Sarah*, schooner ashore and wrecked at Santa Cruz

September __, 1867—*Flying Mist*, schooner, wrecked at Bowen's Landing

December __, 1867—*Eliza Walker*, schooner, lost off the Northern California coast

December 10, 1867—*Anna R. Forbes*, schooner, sank near Red Rock

December 18, 1867—*Kaluna*, schooner, foundered off Shelter Cove

December 23, 1867—*E.C. Long*, sloop, capsized on the San Francisco Bar

1868—*Quaddy Bell*, schooner, wrecked at Mendocino

1868—*L.C. Lane*, schooner, sunk in a collision off Mendocino

January __, 1868—*Kaluna*, schooner, wrecked at Shelter Cove

January 1, 1868—*H.L. Rutgers*, bark, wrecked on Point Bonita

January 13, 1868—*Oliver Cutts*, bark, wrecked on Alcatraz Island

January 20, 1868—*Morning Light*, schooner, lost on the Farallon Islands

January 29, 1868—*Melvina*, schooner, capsized and lost off the Farallon Islands

February 21, 1868—*S.F. Blunt*, schooner, lost at Drake's Bay

March 7, 1868—*Viscata*, ship, wrecked on Baker Beach

March 13, 1868—*Independence*, sloop, lost in a collision near the Farallons

March 14, 1868—*Patta*, schooner, wrecked at Santa Barbara

March 16, 1868—*Columbia*, schooner, wrecked at Cuffey's Cove

April 8, 1868—*Autocrat*, ship, lost on Arch Rock

August 19, 1868—*Commodore*, steamer, sank in a collision in San Francisco Bay

September 1, 1868—*A.J. Burr*, schooner, foundered north of the Farallon Islands

September 3, 1868—*Brignardello*, ship, wrecked near the Cliff House

November __, 1868—*Ella Florence*, schooner, lost at Kent's Point

November 19, 1868—*Hellespont*, ship, wrecked at Pigeon Point

November 28, 1868—*Alert*, schooner, ashore and lost at Half Moon Bay

December 11, 1868—*Henrietta*, schooner, ashore and wrecked at Tomales

December 28, 1868—*C.P. Heustis*, schooner, capsized and lost off Fort Ross

January 8, 1869—*T. Starr King*, schooner, ashore and wrecked at Albion

January 8, 1869—*A. Crosby*, schooner, foundered off Santa Cruz

January 29, 1869—*Ringleader*, schooner, sank in San Pablo Bay

April 17, 1869—*A.J. Monje*, schooner, ashore and lost at Bowens Landing

May 10, 1869—*Ocean Bird*, sloop, run down and sunk in San Francisco Bay

August 29, 1869—*Harlech Castle*, bark, lost off San Simeon

October __, 1869—*Georgie Woods*, schooner in San Francisco Bay

October 10, 1869—*Alpha*, schooner, aground and wrecked eight miles north of Oakland

October 17, 1869—*Sierra Nevada*, steamer, wrecked near Pedro Blanco

November 18, 1869—*J.J. Fransen*, schooner, lost at the Noyo River

December 23, 1869—*Ajax*, schooner, lost at Mendocino

February 3, 1870—*Emma Adelia*, schooner, burned and lost south of Point San Pablo

February 22, 1870—*Golden City*, steamer, wrecked at Cabo San Lazaro, Baja California

May 25, 1870—*Ann Sophia*, schooner, wrecked off Mendocino

June 12, 1870—*Active*, steamer, wrecked near Cape Mendocino

September 30, 1870—*Stranger*, schooner, wrecked at the mouth of the Salinas River

November 7, 1870—*Robert E. Lee*, schooner, wrecked at Point Arena

November 13, 1870—*Advance*, brig, ashore and lost at Ventura

November 15, 1870—*Florence*, schooner, aground and wrecked at Caspar

November 18, 1870—*Wild Pigeon*, steamer, foundered in Fishermen's Bay

November 24, 1870—*Frederick Williams*, schooner, ashore and lost at Benicia

January 2, 1871—*Tolo*, schooner, aground and wrecked at South Point

January 6, 1871—*Massachusetts*, bark, lost at Scammons Lagoon

February 1, 1871—*Eliza*, sloop, wrecked at Point Lobos

February 20, 1871—*William*, schooner, wrecked at Stewart's Point

March 7, 1871—*Emily Schroeder*, schooner, wrecked at Point Arena

March 21, 1871—*W.F. Bowne*, schooner, ashore and lost at Caspar

March 28, 1871—*Minerva*, schooner, wrecked at Stewart's Point

March 28, 1871—*George Hendrick*, schooner, wrecked at Stewart's Point

May 30, 1871—*Caroline E. Foote*, schooner, ashore and wrecked at Hueneme

August 9, 1871—*Aimer*, schooner, wrecked at the Golden Gate

September 8, 1871—*Solano*, schooner, wrecked on the San Francisco Bar

September 18, 1871—*Annie Sise*, ship, wrecked on South Farallon Island

November 25, 1871—*Live Yankee*, ship, lost off the coast of California

December 16, 1871—*Amanda Ager*, schooner, wrecked and abandoned off Gold Bluff

December 16, 1871—*Ashme*, schooner, wrecked at Gold Bluff

December 18, 1871—*Salinas*, steamer, ashore and wrecked at Point San Pedro

January 7, 1872—*Lina Simpson*, sloop, capsized and sank on the San Francisco Bar

January 10, 1872—*Brilliant*, schooner, ashore and wrecked at Mendocino

January 22, 1872—*Ballard*, schooner, wrecked at Noyo River

January 24, 1872—*Josephine Willcutt*, schooner, ashore and wrecked at Point Lobos

February __, 1872—*Ella Florence*, schooner, wrecked at Kent's Point

February __, 1872—*Fanny Jane*, schooner, lost at Navarro

February 21–22, 1872—*Fannie Jane*, schooner, lost at Navarro

February 21–22, 1872—*Meldone*, schooner, lost at French Cove

February 21–22, 1872—*Theresa B. Free*, schooner, lost at Point Arena

February 27, 1872—*Liberty*, schooner, stranded and lost at Timber Cove

April 10, 1872—*Emma Adelia*, schooner, capsized and lost off Duncan's Landing

April 13, 1872—*Hannah Louise*, schooner, capsized and lost at Russian Gulch

April 21, 1872—*C.A. Drew*, schooner, ashore and wrecked at Albion

June 12, 1872—*Golden Rule*, schooner, ashore and wrecked at Albion

June 28, 1872—*Otsego*, schooner, ashore and wrecked at Morro Bay

October 17, 1872—*Acuelo*, ship, ashore and wrecked at Point Montara

November __, 1872—*Lizzie Shea*, schooner, ashore south of Petrolia, Humboldt County

December 5, 1872—*Sacramento*, steamer, wrecked on San Geronimo Island, Baja California

January 21, 1873—*Sovereign*, schooner, lost at the Navarro River

February 7, 1873—*William L. Mighels*, schooner, sunk in collision off Point Bonita

February 28, 1873—*Patrician*, ship, lost on the Golden Gate Bar

June 17, 1873—*Golden Gate*, schooner, wrecked at Morro Bay

June 21, 1873—*Minnie G. Atkins*, schooner, lost on the San Francisco Bar

August 27, 1873—*J.E. Haskins*, schooner, capsized and sank off Point Reyes

September 18, 1873—*Diablo*, steamship, wrecked at Point Loma

December 10, 1873—*Annie Iverson*, schooner, ashore and lost at Point Arena

1874—*Elida*, schooner, lost off the coast of Northern California

February __, 1874—*H. Caroline*, schooner, wrecked at Tomales Bay

March 28, 1874—*J. Mora Moss*, schooner, lost off Stewart's Point

April 2, 1874—*Cora*, schooner, wrecked at Caspar

April 4, 1874—*Golden Rule*, schooner, sank after collision in San Francisco Bay

June 14, 1874—*Prince Alfred*, steamer, wrecked at Potato Cove

June 18, 1874—*Alessandro*, schooner, lost near the Farallons

July 18, 1874—*Falmouth*, schooner, foundered off Point Sur

July 20, 1874—*Warrior Queen*, ship, ashore and wrecked near the Golden Gate

September __, 1874—*Emily Franssen*, schooner, wrecked at Westport

October 3, 1874—*Rescue*, steam tug, wrecked at Point Bonita

November __, 1874—*Emily R. Farnham*, schooner, capsized and lost off the coast of Northern California.

January __, 1875—*Matilda Heron*, schooner, wrecked at Stewarts Point

January 20, 1875—*Curlew*, brig, abandoned and wrecked at Point Arena

January 26, 1875—*Star of the Union*, schooner, sunk in San Francisco Bay

February 1, 1875—*San Ramon*, steamer, ashore and lost at Half Moon Bay

April 18, 1875—*Albert and Edward*, schooner, capsized and lost on the Humboldt Bar

April 20, 1875—*Ventura*, steamer, aground and lost at Monterey

May 1, 1875—*Glenarm*, schooner, wrecked at the mouth of the Russian River

June 17, 1875—*Champlain*, ship, lost on the Farallon Islands

July 3, 1875—*Silas Coombs*, schooner, wrecked at Little River

July 23, 1875—*Eastport*, steamer, wrecked north of Point Arena

July 25, 1875—*Clara R. Sutil*, bark, sank just beyond the Golden Gate

August 14, 1875—*L.R. Whitney*, schooner, wrecked at Noyo River

October __, 1875—*Sunshine*, schooner, disappeared after clearing the Golden Gate

November 11, 1875—*Sarah Louise*, schooner, ashore and lost north of Bodega

December 4, 1875—*Lucy Ann*, brig, ashore and wrecked at San Buenaventura

December 29, 1875—*Elvinia*, schooner, ashore and wrecked at Caspar

January 22, 1876—*West Wind*, scow schooner, sunk in San Francisco Bay

January 23, 1876—*Carolita*, schooner, stranded at Fisk's Mill

February 8, 1876—*Koloa*, brig, ashore and wrecked at San Pedro

February 15, 1876—*Arizona*, schooner, lost at Bridgeport

February 25, 1876—*Kalorama*, steamer, ashore and lost at San Buenaventura

March 9, 1876—*Isaac Jeanes*, bark, wrecked near Fort Point

March 29, 1876—*Crimea*, brig, wrecked at San Buenaventura

April 8, 1876—*Nicholas Biddle*, bark, ashore and lost at Anaheim Landing

May 7, 1876—*Anastasia*, schooner, sank after collision in Suisun Bay

June 7, 1876—*Leader*, schooner, wrecked on San Miguel Island

October 11, 1876—*Annie Stoeffer*, schooner, wrecked at Caspar

October 18, 1876—*Rydal Hall*, ship, aground and wrecked at Pigeon Point

October 24, 1876—*Fideliter*, schooner, lost at Cuffey's Cove

November 23, 1876—*Silver Cloud*, schooner, stranded and lost at Monterey Bay

1877—*Johanna*, schooner, lost off the coast of Mendocino

January __, 1877—*Uncle Abe*, schooner, ashore and wrecked at Point San Quentin

February 26, 1877—*Artful Dodger*, schooner, wrecked at Bowen's Landing

March 25, 1877—*Challenge*, schooner, wrecked at Morro Bay

March 30, 1877—*Frank Jones*, ship, wrecked off Fort Point

April 1, 1877—*Centennial*, schooner, wrecked on the Humboldt Bar

April 27, 1877—*Morning Star*, schooner, capsized and lost off Point Reyes

September 11, 1877—*Anne*, schooner, wrecked Rough & Ready

September 23, 1877—*William Wood*, schooner, burned and sank at Merchantman's Slough

October 4, 1877—*Selma*, schooner, wrecked at Point Reyes

October 5, 1877—*Nautilus*, schooner, stranded and wrecked at Salt Point

October 26, 1877—*Johanne*, schooner, ashore and wrecked at Little River

October 27, 1877—*Clinton*, steamer, sunk in a collision off Arch Rock

November 4, 1877—*Martha and Elizabeth*, schooner, wrecked at Bowen's Landing

November 16, 1877—*Mary Cleveland*, schooner, ashore at Noyo

November 23, 1877—*Albert and Edward*, schooner, wrecked at Salmon Creek

November 26, 1877—*Eden*, schooner, capsized and lost off Point Reyes

December 12, 1877—*Continental*, steamer, wrecked at Eel River

December 16, 1877—*Marietta*, schooner, wrecked on Humboldt Bar

December 23, 1877—*B.F. Lee*, schooner, sunk in a collision at Cuffey's Cove

Curious San Franciscans gather to view the ship *Frank Jones* on the rocks near Fort Point, March 30, 1877. *Courtesy of the San Francisco Maritime NHP.*

1878—*A.P. Jordan*, schooner, lost at Mendocino

January 12, 1878—*Sarah A. Owens*, schooner, wrecked at Mendocino

January 15, 1878—*Reliance*, schooner, wrecked at Goleta

January 16, 1878—*Free Trade*, schooner, ashore and lost at Drake's Bay

January 17, 1878—*Lola*, schooner, ashore and wrecked at Trinidad

January 22, 1878—*Susan A. Owen*, schooner, stranded at Big River

January 25, 1878—*King Philip*, bark, wrecked on Ocean Beach

February __, 1878—*Lime Point*, scow schooner, wrecked at Lime Point

February __, 1878—*Twin Sisters*, schooner, wrecked at Trinidad

February 20, 1878—*Fourth of July*, schooner, ashore and wrecked at Point Reyes

March __, 1878—*General Miller*, schooner, capsized and sank off Tomales

March 24, 1878—*J.P. Haven*, schooner, foundered south of Tomales

April __, 1878—*George P. Haub*, schooner, lost off the coast of Northern California

May 3, 1878—*Hamlet*, ship, sank in San Francisco Bay

June 29, 1878—*U.S. Nelson*, schooner, wrecked near Cape Mendocino

July 9, 1878—*Western Shore*, ship, wrecked on Duxbury Reef

September 28, 1878—*Mary Hart*, schooner, foundered at Bowen's Landing

October 13, 1878—*J.F. Lunt*, schooner, wrecked at Navarro

November 25, 1878—*Laura Pike*, schooner, aground and wrecked at Eureka

January 15, 1879—*Echo*, schooner, foundered and sank off Redwood City

January 20, 1879—*Johanna M. Brock*, schooner, lost on the Humboldt Bar

March 30, 1879—*H.C. Almy*, schooner, wrecked at Bolinas

April 2, 1879—*Francis*, schooner, ashore and lost at Point Reyes

April 16, 1879—*Ellen J. McKinnon*, schooner, capsized and lost off Point Reyes

June 20, 1879—*Annie H. Johnson*, schooner, aground and lost south of Santa Cruz

August 15, 1879—*G.W. Prescott*, schooner, aground and wrecked on San Miguel Island

September 9, 1879—*Emily Franssen*, schooner, wrecked at Westport

October 6, 1879—*Norman*, sloop, ashore and wrecked near Berkeley

October 11, 1879—*Annie Stoffer*, schooner, wrecked at Caspar

November 9, 1879—*Julia Brown*, schooner, ashore and wrecked at Santa Cruz

November 11, 1879—*May Queen*, schooner, wrecked at Crescent City

December 18, 1879—*Mary D. Pomeroy*, schooner, wrecked off Point Reyes

December 20, 1879—*Adelaide Cooper*, bark, ashore and wrecked at San Pedro

1880—*Barbara Fritchie*, schooner, wrecked at Point Arena

1880—*Northwestern*, schooner, capsized and sank off Mendocino

1880—*Osceola*, scow schooner, wrecked off Cape Mendocino

January 11, 1880—*Whipple*, sloop, wrecked on Bed Rock

January 21, 1880—*Confidence*, pilot schooner, lost on Mile Rock

January 22, 1880—*California*, schooner, wrecked at Bowen's Landing

February 4, 1880—*Northwestern*, schooner, wrecked at Little River

February 14, 1880—*Rough and Ready*, schooner, sank in Suisun Bay

April 20, 1880—*Christina Stevens*, schooner, wrecked at Timber Cove

April 21, 1880—*P.A. Owens*, schooner, lost at Black Point, San Francisco Bay

May 21, 1880—*Joseph*, schooner, wrecked at Bodega Head

May 28, 1880—*Monterey*, steamer, ashore and wrecked south of Fort Ross

August 20, 1880—*Energetic*, scow schooner, capsized and sank in San Francisco Bay

August 27, 1880—*Nicholas Van Bergen*, schooner, ashore and wrecked at Smith River

September 13, 1880—*Erin's Star*, bark, wrecked at Point Reyes

October 1, 1880—*Three Sisters*, schooner, wrecked at Gualala

October 5, 1880—*Eliza Miller*, schooner, wrecked at Point Arena

October 23, 1880—*W.H. Hawley*, schooner, wrecked on Ocean Beach

October 27, 1880—*Ada May*, schooner, aground and wrecked at Point Montara

December __, 1880—*Governor Perkins*, schooner, foundered off Cambria

December __, 1880—*Evening Star*, schooner, wrecked at Point Reyes

December __, 1880—*Hyde*, schooner, wrecked off Point Arena

December 2, 1880—*Taffie*, schooner, foundered off Santa Barbara

December 22, 1880—*David & Ettie*, schooner, lost at Cuffey's Cove

December 22, 1880—*Oceaola*, schooner, wrecked at Rough and Ready

December 22, 1880—*Cossack*, schooner, wrecked at Fish Rock

January 25, 1881—*Venus*, schooner, ashore and wrecked on Navarro Beach

February 2, 1881—*Free Trade*, schooner, wrecked at Noyo

March 13, 1881—*Surprise*, schooner, ashore and lost on San Miguel Island

April 26, 1881—*Elko*, schooner, lost at Land's End

June 19, 1881—*Escambia*, steamer, lost on the San Francisco Bar

June 24, 1881—*Franconia*, ship, wrecked on South Farallon Island

September __, 1881—*Alice D. Snow*, ship, lost off the Southern California coast

September 9, 1881—*Transit*, steamship, rammed and sunk in San Francisco Bay

September 26, 1881—*Alice Buck*, ship, ashore and lost at Half Moon Bay

October __, 1881—*Friedeberg*, ship, sank at Oakland Wharf

October 28, 1881—*Penelope*, schooner, lost off Cabo San Lucas, Baja California

January __, 1882—*Constantine*, schooner, ashore and wrecked at Cuffey's Cove

January __, 1882—*Rainier*, steam schooner, lost off the coast of Humboldt

January 9, 1882—*Sparkling Sea*, schooner, aground and wrecked at Westport

January 12, 1882—*Amie*, bark, ashore and wrecked near San Pedro

March 8, 1882—*George Louis*, schooner, wrecked near Mile Rock

March 16, 1882—*Mary Zephyr*, schooner, wrecked on the Mendocino Coast

April 5, 1882—*H.L. Tiernan*, schooner, ashore and wrecked at Lime Point

June 19, 1882—*Escambia*, screw steamer, wrecked on the Farallon Islands

June 20, 1882—*Great Western*, bark, burned to the waterline at Oakland

June 27, 1882—*Lammermoor*, ship, wrecked near Bodega Bay

July 5, 1882—*Galatea*, schooner, foundered several miles off the Golden Gate

August 30, 1882—*Dublin*, bark, aground and wrecked on Ocean Beach

October 5, 1882—*Emily Stevens*, schooner, capsized and wrecked south of Navarro

October 16, 1882—*Bremen*, ship, wrecked on the Farallon Islands

December 20, 1882—*N.L. Drew*, schooner, wrecked at Little River

1883—*Elia Adelia*, schooner, wrecked at Mendocino

March 30, 1883—*Olivia Schultz*, schooner, ashore and wrecked at Rough and Ready

April 8, 1883—*Gussie Klose*, schooner, wrecked at Rockport

April 8, 1883—*William Ackmann*, steam schooner, ashore and wrecked at Point Reyes

April 13, 1883—*Cora*, bark, wrecked at Caspar

April 17, 1883—*Two Brothers*, schooner, capsized and lost off Bodega Head

May 25, 1883—*Pilot*, steamer, sank after explosion at Lakeville

September __, 1883—*Windemere*, bark, ashore and wrecked at Fort Ross

September 7, 1883—*Alviso*, schooner, wrecked at Mendocino

October 5, 1883—*Enterprise*, steamer, wrecked at Crescent City

November __, 1883—*Don Leandro*, schooner, wrecked south of Little River

December 10, 1883—*Kitty Stevens*, schooner, ashore and wrecked at Albion

December 10, 1883—*Lottie Collins*, schooner, ashore and wrecked at Bowen's Landing

December 10, 1883—*R.R. Handy*, schooner, wrecked at Signal Cove

February 15, 1884—*Charles G. White*, steam schooner, ashore and wrecked at Bridgeport

August 6, 1884—*Ellen Adelia*, schooner, lost off Point Reyes

September 27, 1884—*Julius H. Ray*, schooner, wrecked near Point Conception

December 23, 1884—*Lizzie Merrill*, schooner, wrecked at Whitesboro

1885—*John and Samuel*, schooner, wrecked off the coast of Mendocino

1885—*Lulu*, schooner, wrecked at Mendocino

January 22, 1885—*Reliance*, schooner, wrecked at Point Arena

February 2, 1885—*Little River*, schooner, wrecked at Whitesboro

February 15, 1885—*Charles T. Winslow*, schooner, lost on Stewart's Point

March 7, 1885—*J.H. Congden*, schooner, sunk in a collision off Point Reyes

March 19, 1885—*Agnes Nicholaysen*, schooner, lost at Little River

June 6, 1885—*Annie Hermine*, schooner, wrecked at Cape Mendocino

August 8, 1885—*Perseverance*, schooner, wrecked at Tomales Bay

August 20, 1885—*Haddingtonshire*, ship, ashore and lost at Point Reyes

August 26, 1885—*Prescott*, schooner, wrecked on San Miguel Island

September 8, 1885—*Alexander Duncan*, steamer, ashore and wrecked on Mile Rock

September 17, 1885—*Lulu*, schooner, wrecked at Westport

September 30, 1885—*Humboldt*, schooner, wrecked at Westport

September 30, 1885—*Sea Foam*, schooner, wrecked at Westport

October 28, 1885—*D.C. Haskins*, schooner, ashore and wrecked at Russian Landing

November __, 1885—*Hannah Madison*, schooner, ashore and wrecked at Navarro

November __, 1885—*Mendocino*, schooner, wrecked at Whitesboro

November 21, 1885—*Isabel*, sloop, foundered off San Miguel Island

November 24, 1885—*Fairy Queen*, schooner, wrecked at Whitesboro

November 24, 1885—*Maxim*, schooner, lost at Caspar

November 28, 1885—*Lizzie Madison*, schooner, lost at Navarro

December 25, 1885—*Lili of Elsfeith*, bark, wrecked near Humboldt Bay

January 20, 1886—*Alfred*, schooner, lost at Mendocino

January 20, 1886—*Reliance*, schooner, wrecked at Point Arena

March 7, 1886—*J.H. Congden*, schooner, capsized and sank after a collision near Point Reyes

June 23, 1886—*Restless*, schooner, wrecked at Crescent City

September 14, 1886—*Lizzie B. Adams*, schooner, capsized and lost in San Francisco Bay

September 19, 1886—*Unknown*, schooner, ashore and lost at Point Reyes

November 15, 1886—*Union Forever*, schooner, wrecked at Trinidad

December 7, 1886—*Elsie Iverson*, schooner, ashore and wrecked at Point Arena

December 10, 1886—*Fannie A. Hyde*, schooner, wrecked at Point Arena

December 16, 1886—*Truckee*, schooner, wrecked at Albion

December 17, 1886—*Atlantic*, bark, wrecked below the Cliff House

December 17, 1886—*Mary & Ellen*, steam whaler, lost after explosion at San Francisco

January 12, 1887—*Parallel*, schooner, wrecked on Ocean Beach

January 27, 1887—*Georgia R. Higgins*, schooner, wrecked at Whitesboro

February 8, 1887—*America*, ship, wrecked at San Pedro

February 14, 1887—*Kennebec*, bark, ashore and wrecked at San Pedro

February 14, 1887—*San Luis*, barkentine, ashore at Point Fermin

April 4, 1887—*J. Eppinger*, schooner, wrecked at Fort Ross

April 10, 1887—*J.W. Seaver*, bark, wrecked at Point Anno Nuevo

April 15, 1887—*Joshua Grindle*, schooner, ashore and wrecked at Pismo Beach

May 8, 1887—*Champion*, schooner, wrecked at the Albion River

June 14, 1887—*C.H. Merithew*, schooner, wrecked at Westport

June 14, 1887—*Montezuma*, schooner, ashore and wrecked at Ballona Creek

July 3, 1887—*William Frederick*, schooner, ashore and wrecked south of the Cliff House

October 6, 1887—*H.H. Briggs*, schooner, aground and lost at Westport

October 6, 1887—*H.H. Knapp*, schooner, aground and lost at Westport

October 24, 1887—*Caroline Medan*, schooner, lost at Russian Gulch

November 16, 1887—*Mary Cleveland*, schooner, wrecked at Noyo

December 4, 1887—*Mary & Gilbert*, schooner, ashore and wrecked at Albion

December 21, 1887—*San Vicente*, steamer, burned and lost off Pigeon Point

December 27, 1887—*Irma*, schooner, lost at Whitesboro

January 2, 1888—*Z.B. Heywood*, schooner, wrecked at Navarro River

January 2, 1888—*California*, schooner, ashore and wrecked at Bowen's Landing

January 5, 1888—*T.H. Allen*, pilot schooner, capsized and lost on the San Francisco Bar

January 22, 1888—*Claus Spreckels*, brig, wrecked on Duxbury Reef

February 4, 1888—*H. Bendel*, schooner, driven ashore and wrecked on Fish Rock

February 8, 1888—*Gualala*, schooner, ashore and wrecked at Ventura

February 15, 1888—*Charles T. Winslow*, schooner, wrecked at Stewart's Point

February 19, 1888—*Dolphin*, steam tug, foundered off The Heads

March 4, 1888—*Alice Garratt*, steamer, capsized and lost in San Francisco Bay

July 8, 1888—*Bella Vista*, bark, abandoned and sank off Point Reyes

July 9, 1888—*D.C. Murray*, bark, ashore and wrecked at Redondo Beach

July 28, 1888—*Otago*, bark, wrecked at Point Reyes

August 20, 1888—*Energetic*, scow schooner, capsized and lost in San Francisco Bay

August 22, 1888—*City of Chester*, steamer, rammed and sunk off Fort Point

September 12, 1888—*Bessie Everding*, schooner, wrecked near the Cliff House

September 14, 1888—*Scio Page*, schooner. wrecked at Point Reyes

September 15, 1888—*Aeriel*, schooner, lost at Fish Rock, near Point Arena

September 19, 1888—*Pet*, schooner, lost on the North Head of San Francisco Bay

September 27, 1888—*Respigadera*, ship, wrecked at Point Fermin

October 4, 1888—*Elsie Iverson*, schooner, wrecked near Point Reyes Light

November 15, 1888—*Charles T. Winslow*, schooner, wrecked at Stewart's Point

December 23, 1888—*Mendocino*, steam schooner, wrecked on the Humboldt Bar

February 24, 1889—*General Ord*, schooner, aground and lost at Point Arena

March 27, 1889—*Charlotte*, schooner, wrecked on Fish Rock

May __, 1889—*Maggie Young*, schooner, ashore and wrecked at the Russian River

May 7, 1889—*Wing and Wing*, schooner, wrecked at Crescent City

May 7, 1889—*Elvenia*, schooner, wrecked at Crescent City

May 18, 1889—*Golden Gate*, schooner, wrecked at Mendocino

June 25, 1889—*W.L. Hardison*, steamship, burned and sank at Santa Barbara

July 7, 1889—*Collaroy*, barkentine, lost north of the Humboldt River Bar

August 7, 1889—*Adelaide*, schooner, wrecked at Iverson's Landing

August 26, 1889—*Armenia*, ship, burned and sank near Benecia

August 26, 1889—*Honuwar*, ship, burned and sank near Benecia

September 13, 1889—*Page*, schooner, wrecked at Point Reye

October 6, 1889—*William Sparks*, schooner, wrecked at New Haven

November 16, 1889—*Fidelity*, schooner, capsized and lost on the Humboldt River Bar

November 16, 1889—*Caesar Bruns*, schooner, wrecked at Hueneme

December 6, 1889—*Albert Walter*, schooner, abandoned and wrecked at Point Arena

December 14, 1889—*Truckee*, schooner, ashore and lost at Lompoc

January __, 1890—*Ellen Adelia*, schooner, wrecked at Bowen's Landing

January __, 1890—*Dorinda*, sloop, lost at Ensenada

July 3, 1890—*Napa City*, schooner, capsized and sank off Point Arena

September 18, 1890—*Ajax*, steamer, lost on Blunt's Reef

Curious locals examine the barkentine *Collaroy*, ashore and wrecked five miles north of the Humboldt Light, July 7, 1889. *Courtesy of the Special Collections Library, Humboldt State University.*

Riding high in the water, the *Ajax* (foreground) takes on provisions at San Francisco's Greenwich Street Wharf. *Courtesy of the Golden Gate NRA.*

November 4, 1890—*American Boy*, schooner, lost on North Farallon Island

November 4, 1890—*Argonaut*, schooner, on the rocks and lost south of Point Montara

November 12, 1890—*Aleut*, steam tug, ashore and wrecked at Catalina Island

December 2, 1890—*Ida Florence*, schooner, ashore and wrecked at Iverson's Landing

December 3, 1890—*Abbie*, schooner, ashore and wrecked at Caspar

December 4, 1890—*Undine*, steam schooner, sunk off Santa Barbara

December 4, 1890—*South Coast*, schooner, wrecked at Fort Bragg

January 25, 1891—*Venus*, schooner, wrecked at Navarro Beach

February __, 1891—*Lizzie Derby*, schooner, wrecked at Drake's Bay

February 8, 1891—*Fawn*, sloop, ashore and lost on Catalina Island

February 21, 1891—*Elizabeth*, ship, wrecked north of Point Bonita

February 22, 1891—*Theresa B. Free*, schooner, wrecked at Point Arena

June 21, 1891—*Nellie*, schooner, wrecked at Point Vicente

June 26, 1891—*Palestine*, ship, lost on the Farallon Islands

December 21, 1891—*West Coast*, screw steamer, aground and lost at Point Arena

December 29, 1891—*Whiteboro*, steamer, wrecked at Little River

March 27, 1892—*Ventura*, steamer, wrecked at Rockport

August 23, 1892—*Maggie Ross*, steamer, lost at Fort Ross

September 12, 1892—*Golden Horn*, bark, aground and wrecked on Santa Rosa Island

September 26, 1892—*Esperanza*, schooner, wrecked on Duxbury Reef

October 26, 1892—*Joseph S. Spinney*, ship, wrecked at Fort Ross

December 2, 1892—*Barbara*, schooner, wrecked at Shelter Cove

March __, 1893—*King James*, bark, abandoned and lost off Point Conception

March 10, 1893—*Gem*, schooner, wrecked near Fort Point

March 11, 1893—*Gussie Klose*, schooner, wrecked at Mendocino

March 12, 1893—*John McCullough*, schooner, lost on the rocks at Point Arena

May 11, 1893—*Ruth*, schooner, wrecked at Bihler's Point

June 15, 1893—*Bill the Butcher*, schooner, wrecked at Bowen's Landing

October 12, 1893—*Albion*, steamer, aground and lost at Mendocino

October 14, 1893—*Newbern*, steamer, lost on the rocks near Point Fermin

October 26, 1893—*City of New York*, steamer, wrecked off Point Bonita

November 23, 1893—*Gosford*, ship, burned out and sank off Point Conception

April 24, 1894—*Los Angeles*, steamer, lost on the rocks at Point Sur

July 26, 1894—*Rio Rey*, schooner, ashore and wrecked at Point Reyes

October 15, 1894—*Portia*, schooner, wrecked at Stewart's Point

October 16, 1894—*Electra*, schooner, ashore and wrecked at Cambria

October 17, 1894—*Chetco*, schooner, wrecked at Needle Rock

November 2, 1894—*Silver Spring*, steam schooner, wrecked at Rockport

November 8, 1894—*Crown of England*, steam collier, wrecked on Santa Rosa Island

December 11, 1894—*William L. Beebe*, schooner, wrecked near Point Lobos

January 3, 1895—*Samson*, salvage steamer, wrecked at Point Bonita

June 21, 1895—*Rachel*, schooner, stranded and lost north of Point Reyes

July__, 1895—*Restless*, sloop, lost near Santa Cruz Island

August 19, 1895—*James Townsend*, schooner, wrecked at Point Arena

September 18, 1895—*Humboldt*, steamer, wrecked at Punta Gorda

January __, 1896—*Discovery*, bark, lost of the Northern California coast

July 14, 1896—*Colombia*, steamer, wrecked at Pigeon Point

August 8, 1896—*St. Paul*, steamer, wrecked at Point Joe

November __, 1896—*Minnehaha*, schooner, wrecked at Ensenada, Baja California

November 22, 1896—*San Benito*, collier, wrecked near Point Reyes

April 11, 1897—*Yaquina*, steam schooner, aground and wrecked at Hueneme

April 30, 1897—*Alvina*, schooner, ashore and lost at Caspar

May 19, 1897—*California*, schooner, wrecked at Mendocino

May 19, 1897—*Champion*, schooner, wrecked at Albion

October 22, 1897—*Caspar*, steam schooner, wrecked on Saunders Reef

October 22, 1897—*Elnorah*, schooner, run down and sunk off Cape Mendocino

December 2, 1897—*Annie Gee*, schooner, wrecked at Redondo Beach

December 17, 1897—*Wahlberg*, schooner, wrecked at Lagoon Heads, Baja California

The "old tub" *St. Paul*, lost on the south coast of the Monterey Peninsula, August 8, 1896. *Courtesy of the Pacific Grove Museum of Natural History.*

January 19, 1898—*Christina Steffins*, schooner, sank while under tow off Timber Cove

March __, 1898—*Forest Queen*, bark, capsized and lost off the coast of Central California

March 13, 1898—*New York*, ship, wrecked at Half Moon Bay

March 20, 1898—*Helen W. Almy*, bark, lost off the coast of Northern California

March 24, 1898—*Bobolink*, schooner, wrecked at Kent's Point

October 6, 1898—*Nautilus*, sloop, lost at Ensenada, Baja California

December 8, 1898—*Helene*, schooner, wrecked on Santa Cruz Island

January 13, 1899—*Jewel*, steam schooner, wrecked near Caspar

March 2, 1899—*Charlotte*, schooner, wrecked at Point Arena

April __, 1899—*William Sparks*, schooner, wrecked at Newhaven

April 4, 1899—*Chilkat*, steamer, wrecked on the Humboldt Bar

August 23, 1899—*Magic*, gasoline schooner, wrecked on Santa Rosa Island

October __, 1899—*American Girl*, schooner, disappeared after clearing the Golden Gate

November 11, 1899—*Norma*, schooner, wrecked at Fort Bragg

November 24, 1899—*Santa Rosa*, schooner, aground and wrecked on Santa Rosa Island

November 30, 1899—*Eureka*, schooner, wrecked at the Coquille River

December 1, 1899—*Weott*, steamer, wrecked at Humboldt

December 29, 1899—*Unknown*, scow schooner, burned and sunk at Robert's Landing

February 6, 1900—*Nettie Low*, gasoline schooner, capsized and lost off Bolinas Bay

February 6, 1900—*Josie*, schooner, ashore and lost at Coyote Point

March 19, 1900—*City of Florence*, ship, lost at Half Moon Bay

July 21, 1900—*Bonita*, pilot schooner, lost off the Farallon Islands

July 25, 1900—*Laguna*, schooner, wrecked at Golds Bluff

August 10, 1900—*Neptune*, schooner, ashore and wrecked near the Ocean House

September 8, 1900—*May Flint*, bark, sank in San Francisco Bay

October 24, 1900—*Sunol*, steamer, wrecked at Little River

October 24, 1900—*Five Brothers*, schooner, ashore and wrecked near Drake's Bay

November 20, 1900—*D.W. Tietsen*, schooner, wrecked near Bodega Bay

November 20, 1900—*Daisy Rowe*, schooner, ashore and wrecked west of Point Diablo

December 8, 1900—*Cleone*, steam schooner, wrecked near Point Gorda

January 24, 1901—*Barbara Hernster*, schooner, wrecked at Point Arena

February __, 1901—*Dawn*, schooner, wrecked on Anacapa Island

February 21, 1901—*City of Rio de Janeiro*, steamer, lost at the Golden Gate

June 8, 1901—*Francine*, schooner, wrecked on Gull Rock, Santa Cruz Island

August 15, 1901—*Aloha*, steam schooner, burned out and sank in San Francisco Bay

September 1, 1901—*Morning Star*, schooner, ashore and wrecked at Redondo

October 18, 1901—*La Gironde*, schooner, stranded and lost on San Nicolas Island

November 30, 1901—*San Rafael*, steamer, lost in collision near Alcatraz Island

1902—*Bettie Danielson*, scow schooner, wrecked at Mendocino

January 3, 1902—*Walla Walla*, steamer, rammed and sank off Mendocino

February 7, 1902—*Laura Pike*, schooner, abandoned off Cape Mendocino

February 9, 1902—*Occidental*, schooner, wrecked at China Flat, Humboldt County

March 13, 1902—*Reporter*, schooner, wrecked on Ocean Beach

The steam schooner *Weott* was lost on December 1, 1899, near Humboldt Bay. Charles Reiner, her second officer, was awarded a Gold Life Saving Medal from the U.S. Treasury Department for his "extreme heroism in saving life" after the ship was wrecked. *Courtesy of the Special Collections Library, Humboldt State University.*

April 6, 1902—*Archie & Fontie*, schooner, wrecked on Fish Rock, near Point Arena

April 9, 1902—*Kate & Annie*, schooner, wrecked on San Miguel Island

June 20, 1902—*Eureka*, schooner, aground and lost at Mussel Rock

January 30, 1903—*Crescent City*, steam schooner, lost on Fish Rock

March 31, 1903—*Davidson*, schooner, wrecked at Iverson's Landing

April 3, 1903 –*Albion River*, steam schooner, stranded and lost at Bodega Head

April 4, 1903—*S. Danielson*, schooner, lost at Iverson's Landing

August 6, 1903—*Copper Queen*, schooner, ashore and wrecked near Point Reyes

September 25, 1903—*Gifford*, bark, wrecked on Mussel Rock

Two survivors of the *City of Rio de Janeiro* speak with a newspaper reporter as others rest on lifejackets and debris washed ashore from the wreck. *Courtesy of the San Francisco Maritime NHP.*

A "strange light" drew the schooner *Reporter* off course and onto the beach three miles south of the Cliff House on March 13, 1902. *Author's collection.*

November 20, 1903—*Francois Coppee*, ship, lost at Bird Rock

December 18, 1903—*Mary Buhne*, schooner, run down and sunk off the Humboldt Bar

March 11, 1904—*Mabel Gray*, schooner, aground and lost at Redondo Beach

May 24, 1904—*Alton*, steamship, foundered and sank at Red Rock

May 24, 1904—*Fannie Adele*, schooner, burned and lost off Sausalito

July 3, 1904—*Harry*, schooner, sank at Mare Island

August 9, 1904—*Sparrow*, schooner, lost on the Humboldt Bar

September 4, 1904—*James A. Garfield*, schooner, ashore five miles south of the Cliff House

September 4, 1904—*Maggie*, steam schooner, aground and lost near the Cliff House

September 23, 1904—*Drumburton*, bark, lost on Point Pedro

December 7, 1904—*Pearl*, schooner, wrecked off the Golden Gate

1905—*Andrew Peterson*, schooner, lost at Mendocino

1905—*Santa Barbara*, steamer, wrecked at Santa Cruz

February 26, 1905—*Mary Etta*, schooner, wrecked at Stewart's Point

April 22, 1905—*Del Norte*, steam schooner, rammed and sunk off the Coquille River Bar

June 11, 1905—*Robert Sudden*, barkentine, wrecked near the mouth of the Santa Inez River

July 12, 1905—USS *Bennington*, gunboat, sank after explosion in San Diego Bay

July 26, 1905—*Tricolor*, steamer, lost off Cape Mendocino

The stately Scottish-built bark *Gifford* came to grief on Mussel Rocks with a cargo of Australian coal on September 25, 1903. The day after the wreck, Captain Alexander Woodside (left), stevedore, and John Bishop of the Fireman's Fund Insurance Co. visited the wreck to see if there was any chance the ship could be salvaged. They left disappointed. *Courtesy of the San Francisco Maritime NHP.*

September 4, 1905—*J.M. Colman*, schooner, wrecked on San Miguel Island

September 27, 1905—*Gipsy*, steam schooner, lost at Monterey

November 21, 1905—*Katie Flickinger*, barkentine, ashore and wrecked in San Pedro Bay

January 11, 1906—*W.H. Kruger*, steam schooner, ashore and lost at Greenwood

March 31, 1906—*Newsboy*, steam schooner, lost on the Humboldt River Bar

June 4, 1906—*Volunteer*, schooner, wrecked off Bodega Head

June 11, 1906—*Corinthian*, schooner, lost in the Humboldt River Bar

July 17, 1906—*Chico*, steamer, ashore and wrecked near Eureka

August 28, 1906—*Celia*, steam schooner, wrecked near Point Joe

October 5, 1906—*Shasta*, steam schooner, lost on the rocks near Point Conception

January __, 1907—*Maxim*, schooner, lost off the coast of Northern California

January 14, 1907—*Sequoia*, steam schooner, lost on the Humboldt Bar

February 6, 1907—*William F. Witzman*, schooner, wrecked on Duxbury Reef

February 8, 1907—*National City*, steam schooner, wrecked at Hermosa

March 1, 1907—*Corona*, steamer, lost on the Humboldt Bar

March 18, 1907—*Pomona*, steamer, wrecked near Fort Ross

May 29, 1907—*Wizard*, steam tug, sunk off Punta Gorda

June 10, 1907—*Alcazar*, steam schooner, lost on Needle Rock near Point Arena

June 19, 1907—*Louis*, schooner, wrecked on South Farallon Island

July 21, 1907—*Columbia*, steamer, lost in a collision off Shelter Cove

August 15, 1907—*Dawn*, schooner, wrecked at Mussel Rock near Trinidad

October 21, 1907—*Queen Christina*, steamer, stranded and wrecked near Crescent City

November 14, 1907—*Berkeley*, steam schooner, burned and sank off Gaviota

December 8, 1907—*Sotoyome*, gasoline schooner, burned out and lost off Eureka

February 2, 1908—*Ella G.*, schooner, wrecked on Santa Rosa Island

March 14, 1908—*Petril*, sloop, foundered off Santa Barbara

March 18, 1908—*Pomona*, steamer, wrecked near Fort Ross

October 8, 1908—*Newberg*, steam schooner, lost at Bodega

January 12, 1909—*Sibyl Marston*, schooner, aground and wrecked near Surf

January 20, 1909—*Ensign*, schooner, aground and lost near Santa Barbara

March 20, 1909—*R.D. Inman*, steam schooner, wrecked at Bolinas

April 26, 1909—*Rhoderick Dhu*, bark, wrecked at Monterey

July 31, 1909—*Winnebago*, steam schooner, wrecked at Point Arena

November 20, 1909—*St. Croix*, lost near Point Dume

December 7, 1909—*Majestic*, steam schooner, ashore and wrecked at Point Sur

May 25, 1910—*Dora Bluhm*, schooner, wrecked on Santa Rosa Island

July 9, 1910—*Annie E. Smale*, schooner, lost on the rocks at Point Reyes

August 2, 1910—*James Rolph*, schooner, wrecked in San Pablo Bay

November 22, 1910—*Selja*, streamer, rammed and sunk off the Golden Gate

April 18, 1911—*Triton*, schooner, sank off Pigeon Point

July 1, 1911—*Sonoma*, schooner, lost at Point Reyes

July 7, 1911—*Santa Rosa*, steamer, wrecked near Point Arguello

August 30, 1911—*Comet*, schooner, lost on San Miguel Island

November 29, 1911—*Florence*, schooner, wrecked at Descanso Bay, Baja California

January __, 1912—*Alsen*, schooner, foundered off Ensenada, Baja California

February 2, 1912—*Ida McKay*, schooner, capsized and lost off Northern California

May 11, 1912—*Mayflower*, schooner, rammed and sunk north of Point Reyes

Her masts and stack askew, the steam schooner *Celia* was impaled on the rocks at Point Joe on the south coast of the Monterey Peninsula. No one was lost or injured in the August 28, 1906 wreck, but the ship was a total loss. *Courtesy of the Pacific Grove Museum of Natural History.*

The Humboldt River Bar claimed the steam schooner *Sequoia* on January 14, 1907. *Courtesy of the Kelley House Museum.*

With the house flag of the Pacific Coast Steamship Company flying at her main mast, the coastal steamer *Pomona* is seen about to dock at Eureka, circa 1907. *Courtesy of the Kelley House Museum.*

June 28, 1912—*Signal*, steamer, wrecked at Point Lobos

August 29, 1912—*Lillebonne*, schooner, capsized and lost at Point Bonita

October 20, 1912—*J.J. Loggie*, steam schooner, wrecked near Point Arguello

November 5, 1912—*Herald*, steamer, burned and later sank in San Francisco Bay

January 28, 1913—*Samoa*, steam schooner, wrecked on Ten-Mile Beach

March 21, 1913—*Albion*, steam schooner, wrecked at Bowen's Landing

April 23, 1913—*Charles Nelson*, steam schooner, burned out at Field's Landing

June 19, 1913—*Riverside*, steamer, lost on Blunt's Reef

June 27, 1913—*Casco*, steam schooner, lost near the Piedras Blancas Light

June 28, 1913—*Signal*, steam schooner, wrecked on the San Francisco Bar

July 12, 1913—*J.H. Lunsmann*, schooner, run down and sunk in San Francisco Bay

August 9, 1913—*Point Arena*, steam schooner, lost at Pigeon Point

September 20, 1913—*Santa Cruz*, steam schooner, wrecked at Rincon Point

October 15, 1913—*Merced*, steam schooner, wrecked at Point Gorda

November 7, 1913—*Colonel Baker*, scow schooner, wrecked at Drake's Bay

December 31, 1913—*Pomo*, steam schooner, wrecked at Point Reyes

January 15, 1914—*Pathfinder*, schooner, wrecked at Point Diablo

January 16, 1914—*Polaris*, schooner, lost on Potato Patch Shoal

April 2, 1914—*Hartley*, steamer, sank at Fisherman's Cove

August 27, 1914—*Scotia*, steamer, ashore and lost near Purisima Point

November 23, 1914—*Hanalei*, steam schooner, wrecked on Duxbury Reef

December 18, 1914—*Coos Bay*, steamer, aground and wrecked near Ventura

January 8, 1915—*Eureka*, steam schooner, wrecked at Point Bonita

April 13, 1915—*Monarch*, steam tug, sank in San Pablo Bay

May 23, 1915—*Aggi*, ship, wrecked on Santa Rosa Island

October 18, 1915—*Alliance*, schooner, foundered north of Point Arena

1916—*James H. Higgins*, steamer, wrecked at Point Hueneme

January 28, 1916—*Aberdeen*, steam schooner, wrecked at Fort Point

February 1, 1916—*Excelsior*, steam schooner, rammed and sunk off Mile Rock

On January 28, 1913, the steam schooner *Samoa* was en route from Caspar to San Francisco when she ran aground in thick fog on Ten-Mile Beach. *Courtesy of the Kelley House Museum.*

March 21, 1916—*Ruby*, schooner, foundered at the Golden Gate

April 8, 1916—*Magnolia*, schooner, wrecked on the Klamath River Bar

May 9, 1916—*Roanoke*, steamer, sank off Port San Luis

June 14, 1916—*Bear*, steamer, wrecked at Cape Mendocino

January 13, 1917—USS *Milwaukee*, cruiser, ashore and lost on Samoa Beach

April 27, 1917—*Coronado*, steam schooner, foundered off Point Arena

May 2, 1917—*Alcatraz*, steam schooner, wrecked on Mile Rock

May 7, 1917—*Trinidad*, steam schooner, sank in Willapa Bay

June 13, 1917—USCGC *McCullough*, cutter, sank after collision off Point Conception.

June 17, 1917—*R.C. Slade*, schooner, ashore and wrecked near Point Arena

July 29, 1917—*Del Norte No. 2*, steamer, stranded and wrecked at Point Arena

October 9, 1917—*Quinault*, steamer, stranded and lost at Punta Gorda

December 17, 1917—USS *F-1*, submarine, sank after collision off San Diego

1918—*W.H. Murphy*, steam schooner, lost off Trinidad

February 10, 1918—*Chetco*, schooner, burned and sank off Santa Barbara

February 26, 1918—*Noyo*, steam schooner, wrecked at Point Arena

May 2, 1918—*Alcatraz*, steam schooner, wrecked near Point Arena

October 27, 1918—*Mandalay*, steam schooner, wrecked near the Klamath River

December 14, 1918—*Sehome*, steamer, lost in a collision at McNears Point

December 19, 1918—*George Loomis*, steamer, wrecked at Blunt's Reef

March 13, 1919—*Ituna*, steamer, foundered near the San Francisco Lightship

April 2, 1919—*Albert*, bark, aground and lost at Point Reyes

September 21, 1919—*North Fork*, steam schooner, stranded and lost at Punta Gorda

December 23, 1919—*Girlie Mahoney*, steam schooner, wrecked at Albion

December 23, 1919—*J.S. Higgins*, schooner, stranded and lost at Albion

August 29, 1920—*Arakan*, steamship, wrecked at Point Reyes

October 10, 1920—*Melvina*, steamer, sank in San Francisco Bay

February 4, 1921—*Klamath*, steamer, ashore and wrecked near Mendocino

A Chronology of Losses

August 6, 1921—*Alaska*, steamer, wrecked on Blunt's Reef

September 14, 1921—*Lotus*, steam schooner, burned out and sunk off Anacapa Island

May 1, 1922—*Whittier*, steam tanker, wrecked on Saunder's Reef

July 5, 1922—*Arctic*, steam schooner, wrecked at Point Arena

September 16, 1922—*Thomas L. Wand*, steam schooner, wrecked near Point Sur

October 7, 1922—*Lyman A. Stewart*, tanker, aground after a collision off Land's End

December 1, 1922—*Orteric*, freighter, wrecked on Sail Rock

December 28, 1922—*Stockton City*, steam schooner, wrecked at Russian Gulch

February 23, 1923—*Watson A. West*, schooner, wrecked on San Miguel Island

March 9, 1923—*Babinda*, steamer, burned out and sunk off Big Sur

May 21, 1923—*Coquille*, steam schooner, ashore and lost on Manchester Beach

September 8, 1923—*Cuba*, passenger steamer, lost off San Miguel Island

September 8, 1923—USS *Fuller*, destroyer, wrecked at Honda Point

September 8, 1923—USS *Woodbury*, destroyer, wrecked at Honda Point

September 8, 1923—USS *Chauncey*, destroyer, wrecked at Honda Point

September 8, 1923—USS *Young*, destroyer, wrecked at Honda Point

September 8, 1923—USS *S.P. Lee*, destroyer, wrecked at Honda Point

September 8, 1923—USS *Nicholas*, destroyer, wrecked at Honda Point

The British freighter *Orteric*, wrecked on Salt Rock with a cargo of sheep, December 1, 1922. *Courtesy of the Kelley House Museum.*

September 8, 1923—USS *Delphy*, destroyer, wrecked at Honda Point

December 14, 1923—*Flavel*, steam schooner, wrecked at Point Cypress

1924—*Cuatemoc*, screw schooner, lost at Mendocino

1924—*Oakland*, schooner, sank off Cape Mendocino

June 24, 1924—*Mary Hanlon*, gasoline schooner, foundered off Cape Mendocino

September 22, 1924—*Miduena*, schooner, wrecked north of False River

October 1, 1924—*La Feliz*, steam schooner, wrecked north of Santa Cruz

October 9, 1924—*Shark*, gas schooner, foundered at Crescent City

1926—*Charles F. Crocker*, bark, foundered off Catalina Island

February 7, 1926—*Yosemite*, steam schooner, wrecked on Ocean Beach

March 9, 1926—*David C. Meyer*, steamer, aground and lost at Point Fermin

August 4, 1926—*Norlina*, steamer, lost on Salt Point

September 30, 1926—*Shasta*, steam schooner, burned out and lost in San Francisco Bay

October 26, 1926—*Everett*, steam schooner, foundered off Table Bluff

October 29, 1926—*Eureka*, steamer, sank after explosion off Eureka

February 13, 1927—*Esther Buhne*, schooner, wrecked at Newport Beach

May 18, 1927—*Indiana Harbor*, steam schooner, wrecked off the coast of Humboldt County

October 27, 1927—*Coos Bay*, lumber carrier, wrecked at Land's End

June 28, 1929—*Hartwood*, steam schooner, wrecked at Point Reyes

August 20, 1929—*Jane L. Stafford*, barkentine, beached on Santa Rosa Island after a collision

August 29, 1929—*San Juan*, steamer, sank after collision off Pigeon Point

November 22, 1929—*Daisy Putnam*, steam schooner, wrecked at Punta Gorda

March 28, 1930—*Rhine Maru*, freighter, wrecked off Big Sur River

May 8, 1930—*Richfield*, tanker, wrecked at Point Reyes

September 16, 1930—*South Coast*, steam schooner, lost off Point Reyes

November 7, 1930—*Munleon*, steamer, wrecked near Point Reyes

November 8, 1930—*Brooklyn*, steam schooner, lost on the Humboldt River Bar

Established in 1874, the Point Fermin Lighthouse was built of California redwood brought south aboard one of California's ubiquitous lumber schooners. *Courtesy of the Port of Los Angeles Archives.*

February 23, 1931—*Sea Foam*, steam schooner, aground and wrecked at Point Arena

April 21, 1931—*Thomas P. Emigh*, schooner, ashore and wrecked at Redondo

May 30, 1931—*Harvard*, passenger steamer, wrecked at Point Arguello

October 23, 1931—*Wilmington*, steamer, sank at Mad River, Humboldt County

February 11, 1932—*Washington*, steamer, foundered in Humboldt Bay

February 24, 1933—*Yellowstone*, steam schooner, ashore and lost in Humboldt Bay

On October 27, 1927, the lumber steamer *Coos Bay* was punctured below the waterline and deemed unsalvageable after going onto the rocks at Land's End near the entrance to San Francisco Bay. *Courtesy of the San Francisco Maritime NHP.*

Built in Aberdeen, Washington, in 1904 by Lindstrom Shipbuilding Company, the steam schooner *Sea Foam* plied the California coastal trades for twenty-six years before she went ashore and was wrecked at Point Arena on February 23, 1931. *Courtesy of the Kelley House Museum.*

March 13, 1933—*Twerton*, steam schooner, lost south of the Humboldt Bar

April 14, 1933—*William H. Smith*, schooner, ashore and wrecked at Monterey

May 28, 1933—*Nippon Maru*, tanker, wrecked at Honda Point

May 28, 1933—*Chehalis*, steam schooner, lost at Point Conception

September 25, 1933—USCGC *256*, Coast Guard cutter, grounded and lost on Spanish Beach

October 5, 1933—*Lahaina*, bark, stranded at Point Vincente

December 28, 1933—*Stockton City*, schooner, wrecked at Russian Gulch

September 2, 1934—*Cornell*, steam schooner, stranded and wrecked at Cypress Point

September 3, 1934—*J.B. Stetson*, steam schooner, wrecked off Monterey

January 18, 1935—*Aurora*, schooner, ashore and wrecked in Monterey Bay

June 10, 1935—*Noyo*, steam schooner, wrecked at Point Arena

1936—*Necanium*, steam schooner, foundered in San Pablo Bay

March 12, 1936—*Indiana*, bark, stranded and lost at Long Beach

October 7, 1936—*Ohioan*, freighter, wrecked at Point Lobos

March 6, 1937—*Frank H. Buck*, tanker, wrecked at Land's End

December __, 1937—*Ellen F.*, salvage ship, wrecked at Land's End

December 7, 1937—USS *Koka*, naval tug, lost on San Clemente Island

October 20, 1938—*Dorothy Wintermote*, steamer, sank under tow off Fort Ross

A superstitious crew blamed the wreck of the *Tiverton* on a "stow away" black cat that had snuck aboard in San Francisco before the steam schooner sailed to her doom in March 1933. *Author's collection.*

Run ashore in a heavy fog on June 10, 1935, the *Noyo*'s crew was saved, but the steam schooner was beyond salvage. *Courtesy of the Kelley House Museum.*

1939—*Daisy*, steam schooner, foundered in Humboldt Bay

September 18, 1939—*Redwood*, steam schooner, exploded and sank off Humboldt

September 24, 1939—*Minnie Caine*, schooner, aground and lost near Santa Monica

1940—*Daisy Matthews*, steam schooner, foundered off Trinidad Head

January 22, 1941—*Katherine Donovan*, steam schooner, lost in Humboldt Bay

December 20, 1941—*Emidio*, tanker, torpedoed and sunk off Cape Mendocino

December 23, 1941—*Montebello*, tanker, torpedoed and sunk off Cambria

June 3, 1942—USS *Bunting*, minesweeper, sunk in collision near Point Diablo

June 30, 1942—USS *Hornbill*, minesweeper, sunk in collision in San Francisco Bay

October 26, 1942—*Larry Doheny*, tanker, torpedoed and sunk off Eureka

November 15, 1942—*Susan Olsen*, steamer, foundered at Point St. George

1943—*Unimak*, steam schooner, lost in San Francisco Bay

May 31, 1944—*Henry Bergh*, freighter, wrecked on South Farallon Island

July 17, 1944—*E.A. Bryan*, freighter, wrecked in an explosion at Port Chicago

July 17, 1944—*Quinault Victory*, freighter, wrecked in an explosion at Port Chicago

August 9, 1944—*F.A. Douty*, steamship, foundered in San Francisco Bay

September 11, 1944—USS *PC-815*, sub chaser, lost in collision off San Diego

March 5, 1945—USS *LCS 127*, landing craft, wrecked at San Pedro

A collision with the passenger liner *President Coolidge* near Point Lobos claimed the tanker *Frank H. Buck* on March 6, 1937. *Courtesy of the Kelley House Museum.*

With her midsection completely blown away, the charred and twisted bow of the Keystone Tankship Corp.'s *Markay* points skyward at her berth at the Port of Los Angeles. *Author's collection.*

May 4, 1945—USS *LCT-1358*, landing craft, wrecked at San Pedro

June 22, 1947—*Markay*, tanker, wrecked in an explosion at the Port of Los Angeles

July 11, 1949—*Ioannis G. Kulukundis*, freighter, wrecked at Point Arguello

September 9, 1949—*Pacific Enterprise*, freighter, wrecked near Point Arena

July 18, 1950—*Point Loma*, steamer, lost on Seal Rock near Crescent City

August 25, 1950—*Benevolence*, hospital ship, sank after a collision off the Golden Gate

July 12, 1952—*Victor H. Kelly*, tanker, exploded and burned at Oleum

December 11, 1952—*Fernstream*, freighter, sank after a collision near the Golden Gate

July 14, 1953—*Jacob Luckenbach*, freighter, sank after a collision off the Golden Gate

May 14, 1956—*Howard Olson*, lumber steamer, sank after collision off the Golden Gate

January 29, 1957—*Jeanny*, tanker, sank after explosion at Alameda

March 13, 1961—*Dominator*, freighter, wrecked at Palos Verdes

April __, 1961—USS *Makassar Strait*, escort carrier, aground and lost on St. Nicholas Island

February 7, 1962—*Chickasaw*, freighter, wrecked on Santa Rosa Island

October 12, 1966—USS *George A. Johnson*, destroyer escort, ashore and wrecked at Pacifica

The Union Oil tanker *Victor H. Kelly* in ballast a few months before a fire and two explosions tore her apart while unloading a cargo of crude oil at San Pedro, July 1952. *Author's collection.*

Several salvage attempts failed to pull the Greek-flag *Dominator* off the rocks at the foot of Palos Verdes, where her rusted bones remain to this day. *Courtesy of Courtney A. White.*

April 13, 1970—*La Janelle*, passenger liner, wrecked at Hueneme

December 17, 1976—*Sansinena*, tanker, sank after explosion at the Port of Los Angeles

October 31, 1984—*Puerto Rican*, tanker, sank after explosion off the Golden Gate

September 2, 1987—*Pacbaroness*, bulk carrier, sank after a collision off Point Conception

BIBLIOGRAPHY

BOOKS

Benson, Richard M. *Steamships and Motorships of the West Coast*. Seattle, WA: Superior Publishing Co., 1968.

Chapelle, Howard M. *The Search for Speed Under Sail, 1700–1885*. New York: W.W. Norton & Co., 1967.

Coman, Edwin T., and Helen M. Gibbs. *Time, Tide and Timber: Over a Century of Pope & Talbot*. Stanford, CA: Stanford University Press, 1949.

Cutler, Carl C. *Greyhounds of the Sea*. Annapolis, MD: Naval Institute Press, 1984.

Delgado, James P. *To California by Sea*. Columbia: University of South Carolina Press, 1990.

Delgado, James P., and Stephen Heller. *Shipwrecks at the Golden Gate*. N.p.: Lexikos, 1989.

Gibbs, James. *Disaster Log of Ships*. New York: Superior Books, 1971.

———. *Pacific Square Riggers*. West Chester, PA: Schiffer Publishing, Ltd., 1987.

————. *Peril at Sea*. West Chester, PA: Schiffer Publishing Ltd., 1986.

————. *Shipwrecks of the Pacific Coast*. Portland, OR: Binford & Mort, 1957.

————. *West Coast Lighthouses*. Seattle, WA: Superior Publishing Co., 1974.

Gleason, Duncan. *The Islands and Ports of California*. New York: Devin-Adair Co., 1958.

Hitchman, James H. *A Maritime History of the Pacific Coast, 1540–1980*. Lanham, MD: University Press of America, 1990.

Jackson, Walter A. *The Doghole Schooners*. Volcano: California Traveler Publications, 1969.

Kemble, John Haskell. *A Hundred Years of Pacific Mail*. Newport News, VA: Mariners Museum, 1950.

————. *San Francisco Bay*. New York: Bonanza Books, 1957.

Krieger, Michael. *Where Rails Meet the Sea*. New York: Michael Friedman Publishing Group, 1998.

Layton, Thomas N. *The Voyage of the* Frolic. Stanford, CA: Stanford University Press, 1997.

Lockwood, Charles A. *Tragedy at Honda*. Washington, D.C.: Naval Institute Press, 1986.

Lubbock, Basil. *The Down Easters*. New York: Dover Publications, 1987.

Marquez, Ernest M. *Port Los Angeles: A Phenomenon of the Railroad Era*. San Marino, CA: Golden West Books, 1975.

Marshall, Don B. *California Shipwrecks*. Seattle, WA: Superior Publishing Co., 1978.

McNairn, Jack, and Jerry MacMullen. *Ships of the Redwood Coast*. Stanford, CA: Stanford University Press, 1945.

Miller, William H. *Doomed Ships: Great Ocean Liner Disasters*. Mineola, NY: Dover Publications, 2006.

Mitchell, Al. *Historic American Lighthouses*. New York: Barnes & Noble Books, 2003.

Newell, Gordon, and Joe Williamson. *Pacific Coastal Liners*. Seattle, WA: Superior Books, 1959.

————. *Pacific Lumber Ships*. New York: Superior Books, 1960.

Niven, John. *The American President Lines and Its Forebears, 1848–1984*. Newark: University of Delaware Press, 1987.

O'Flaherty, Joseph S. *An End and a Beginning: The South Coast and Los Angeles, 1850–1887*. Pasadena, CA: Castle Press, 1992.

————. *Those Powerful Years: The South Coast and Los Angeles, 1887–1917*. Pasadena, CA: Castle Press, 1992.

Sawyer, L.A., and W.H. Mitchell. *The Liberty Ships*. 2nd ed. New York: Lloyd's of London Press, 1985.

————. *Victory Ships and Tankers*. Cambridge, MD: Cornell Maritime Press, 1974.

Semones, JoAnn. *Sea of Troubles: The Lost Ships of Big Sur*. El Cerrito, CA: Glencannon Press, 2012.

Shaw, James L. *Ships of the Panama Canal*. Annapolis, MD: Naval Institute Press, 1985.

Soule, Frank, John H. Gihon and James Nisbet. *The Annals of San Francisco*. Berkeley, CA: Berkeley Press, 1999.

Stindt, Fred A. *Matson's Century of Ships*. San Francisco, CA: privately published, 1991.

Tate, E. Mowbray. *Transpacific Steam*. Cranbury, NJ: Cornwall Books, 1996.

U.S. Government Printing Office. *List of Merchant Vessels of the United States, 1884–1920*. Washington, D.C.

NEWSPAPERS

Amador Ledger
California Star
*Commercial News &
    Shipping Guide*
Daily Alta California
Journal of Commerce
Los Angeles Daily
Los Angeles Daily Express
Los Angeles Herald
*Los Angeles Herald-
    Examiner*
Los Angeles Star
Los Angeles Times
Marin Journal
Mariposa Gazette
New York Times
New York Tribune

Oakland Tribune
Orange County Register
Pacific Marine Review
Pacific Rural Press
Sacramento Daily Union
Sacramento Transcript
San Francisco Bulletin
San Francisco Californian
San Francisco Call
San Francisco Chronicle
Santa Barbara Daily Press
Sausalito News
Times of London
Tombstone Daily Epitaph
Ukiah Republican-Press
Ventura Signal

MAGAZINES

Marine Digest
Marine Engineering Log
Naval Institute Proceedings
Pacific Maritime Review
Pacific Shipper
Sea Classics
Steamboat Bill

INDEX

ABOUT THE AUTHOR

Michael D. White has spent the better part of the last four decades working as an editor and writer covering international trade and transportation for more than a dozen publications and websites. An amateur maritime historian and researcher, this is his fourth nonfiction book. White is a native Southern Californian, served in the U.S. Coast Guard and lives in Los Angeles.